Melva Jane Steen Ph.D.

Sensible Shoes

The Experiences of an Older
Peace Corps Volunteer in Africa

ISBN: 1461095883
ISBN-13: 9781461095880

This book is dedicated to the memory of
Joseph Kafakoma
1979 - 2004

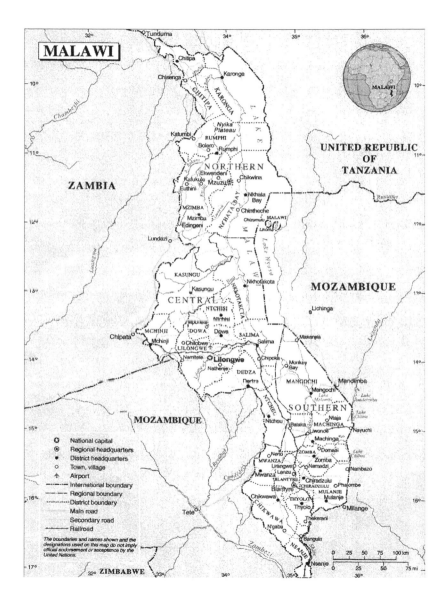

Table of Contents

Introduction

Work had been my life since I was fifteen. I had recently retired from a full-time teaching position at a small university, I was still in good health, and not ready to sit in a rocking chair and knit or play bridge for the rest of my life.

The question I asked myself was, "What should I do with my remaining years?"

This is a question many older, retired persons ask themselves. Like most older persons, I had accumulated a modicum of usable skills over the years, particularly in the health care field. I enjoy working with people. What could I do that would be useful and give me some satisfaction?

My children, grandchildren, and great grandchildren did not need me. I suppose I could have intruded in their lives and made myself useful, but they were all healthy and busily engaged in their own lives. They really did not need me.

After researching a variety of volunteer medical programs, such as Doctors without Borders, both here in the states and overseas, I decided to try for the Peace Corps (PC). Being an independent female activist, I have to admit I did it with a slightly belligerent attitude. I was not prepared to be turned down simply because of my age. I would probably scream "ageism" if I were not accepted.

The literature said that only one person out of every three who applied was accepted into the Peace Corps. This bit of data, while not in my favor, did not deter me.

Luck was on my side, because President Bush was encouraging older people to become volunteers in various organizations, including the Peace Corps. Imagine my surprise when I received a call from the recruiter in my state for an interview over the phone. When the recruiter asked where I preferred to be assigned, my immediate response was "some place warm, preferably Africa." I was posted to Malawi, Africa in the summer of 2003.

The old saying, "Be careful what you ask for, you may get it," echoed in my head. I had never heard of Malawi. What was I getting myself into? None of my immediate friends knew where Malawi was located in Africa.

Africa as a continent had always intrigued me. Perhaps I was an African in a past life? However, the true reason for my interest in Africa was because of a story my grandmother told me when I was a child, about two famous explorers who were supposedly distantly related to our family. Their names were Osa and Martin Johnson. They were early explorers and photographers of Africa. Stories of their adventures and pictures of their safaris in "dark" Africa appeared in *National Geographic* at the turn of the 20th century. In the 30s, their pictures were on cereal boxes, along with Roscoe Turner, the famous lion tamer, and Jack Armstrong, the "All American Boy."

Grandmother told how she bounced Martin on her knee when he was a baby. Later research and comparison of the ages of my grandmother and Martin revealed she must have been about five years old when this event happened!

I was awed by Osa's courage to run away from her home in Chanute, Kansas, leaving behind a safe, secure life, to marry Martin. Considered a "soldier of fortune," he was ten years older than Osa, who was barely 16. The year was 1910. Osa's daring, spirited life intrigued me as an adolescent.

A second reason for choosing Africa was because I wanted to be sent to a warm climate to spend the next twenty-seven months, the time allotted for an assignment in the Peace Corps. I presumed all of Africa was warm.

Malawi is south of the equator; considered sub-Saharan, which makes the seasons the direct opposite of the seasons in North America. I arrived in July which is their coldest time of the year. Not prepared for the cold, I suffered until I became acclimated.

According to information I had been given by the Peace Corps, I knew I would probably be living in a mud nut with no running water or electricity. The thought of such a primitive existence did not bother me. Born in 1928, I was a child of the "great depression." The small farm I grew up on in rural Missouri did not have these amenities until the Rural Electrification Act (REA) was implemented in the late 30's and early 40's. Secretly, I must admit that I felt a little smug because I knew I would have peers who were straight out of college and would have no idea of how to build a fire to cook a meal or exist without running water and electricity for their electronic gadgets. I decided age and experience might have some advantages over youth!!

I will stop here, and the reader will find the rest of my story contained in the letters, and excerpts from my journal descriptions of my life as an older Peace Corps Volunteer. It is my hope that by sharing my story other older/retired persons, also in good health, with a zest for living and wanting to make a contribution to a better world, will be inspired to find the courage to leave the comforts of home and share their accumulated wisdom and life skills with people in another part of this world in which we are all part of "an interconnected web of existence."

The following poem could easily be the mantra for the Peace Corps. It became my purpose for being in Africa.

"Go to the people
Live with them,
Learn from them...

Start with what they know;
Build with what they have.
But, with the best leaders,
When the work is done,
The task accomplished,
The people will say,
We have done this ourselves!"

Lao Tzu (700 BC)

Melva Steen, RN, Ph.D., RPCV (Returned Peace Corps Volunteer)

Chapter One
The Big Decision

There are no "how to" books on making many of life's big decisions. Retirement was the "biggy" I was facing when, at the age of seventy-three, I stepped down as the chair of the Department of Nursing at a small university in Pueblo, Colorado. Up to this point my life had been dictated for me by society, and took me on the same path of most women of my generation. Women had fewer choices for a career in the 30s and 40s. Becoming a nurse, teacher, or secretary were the main choices open to women. I chose nursing, and spent the next fifty years in the health care field. Now, in 2001, I had the opportunity to decide what I wanted to do with the rest of my life. It was like being given the proverbial "30 pieces of silver." How did I want to spend them?

My work in the area of health care began when, at the age of fifteen, while still in high school, I trained as a nurse's aide at a local hospital. I emptied bed pans, bathed patients, helped prepare meals, bathed the newborns and carried them to their mothers, and learned about sterile technique as I catheterized patients, and changed dressings.

Once, when I was standing in the doorway of the operating room while the doctors were performing

1

a caesarian section, I heard a small pop. The doctors, who were busy attending to the patient, did not seem to notice or hear the "pop" as the baby was lifted from the womb. When the newborn was handed to me, I carried it into the nursery and started to bathe it. It was then that I noticed the femur of one small leg was broken. I called this to the attention of the doctors, who placed a cast on the infant's tiny leg.

My experiences as a nurse's aide sealed my plans for my future. Caring for the sick became my calling in life. I wanted to become a doctor, perhaps a pediatrician. However, no one in my immediate family had ever had such aspirations, or even attended a college. I knew money and finding adequate support systems would be a problem. I had to scale back my goals, and I settled for becoming a professional nurse instead.

Father was opposed to my becoming a nurse. He likened a nurse to being a prostitute. "Any woman who has seen the human body and handled it so intimately, as a nurse must do, cannot retain her innocence and purity," was his thinking. The only suitable occupations for a woman, he thought, were as a teacher or secretary. This thinking was common for that time. I knew it would not do any good to seek his support for my goal by asking him for the money for tuition. Instead, I asked my mother to talk to my father to see if she could change his mind. It must have been some talk, because I soon had a check for $150 in my hand; enough to cover my first year's tuition.

With the backing of my mother, I applied and was accepted into a diploma nursing program at St. Luke's School of Nursing in Kansas City, Missouri, at the tender age of seventeen. The year was 1945. World War II had just ended. The government had funded a program during the war to educate more nurses to cover the shortage of nurses brought on by so many nurses who had left civilian nursing and entered the armed services during the war. This program, the Cadet Nurse Program, paid the tuition for nurses at a school of their choosing. The program was due to end in 1945, but, to my joy, it was extended for another year. I had been feeling guilty for asking my father to pay for my tuition when I knew it was not what he wanted for me. I happily returned his check and became a Cadet Nurse. I paid my remaining two years of school by cashing my war bonds. The Cadet program provided me with a small monthly stipend. I became independent, and determined to become emancipated from my family.

My first place of employment was as the night nurse supervisor at the St. Louis State Hospital for the mentally ill. Nurses were still in short supply. I knew I was being placed in a position of responsibility that common sense told me I was not ready for. However, as I was told later, "They had a boat, and needed someone to row it!" That someone was me. The Director of Nursing assured me I could do the job, saying, "You may not always know what to do, but you will know what not to do." With this sage piece of advice ringing in my ears, for the next year I worked the night shift, trudging through the dark tunnels, under the hospital, with my flashlight, to visit each ward. The patients and staff were helpful. Knowing I was very green, they told me what I needed to do!!

One night I was called to the hospital ward where a young girl was having a baby. The girl was obese and mentally retarded. No one knew she was pregnant, not even the patient or her family. She had been given a pass over the New Year holiday and had attended an all night drinking party without her parent's permission or knowledge. Nine months later she delivered a five pound baby boy. I have often wondered what happened to that baby. It was placed in foster care, but would it have a normal growth and development?

In 1949, after supporting myself for a year with my new RN license, and still following the path of the average woman of my era, I met and married the first man who proposed to me. Although I had decided not to get married for at least several more years, maybe never, the message I was receiving from my culture and society was that a single woman, who had reached a certain age, needed to get married and raise a family. That was what you were supposed to do in the next phase of your life! I was twenty-two.

For the next twenty-some years, I followed my husband as he became a career non-com in the Air Force. In order to keep my nursing skills current, I worked part-time between having children. As we moved from base to base and overseas, our first child was born in St. Louis, Missouri, the second in Mobile, Alabama, the third in Sculthorpe, England, and the fourth in Troon, Scotland. The fifth and last child was born in Kansas City, Missouri, when my husband retired.

As a serviceman's wife, it was always my responsibility to pack the household goods and supervise our transfer to the next assignment. Usually this meant staying behind to allow the children to complete a school year.

The experience of traveling to new places, meeting new people, and making new friends was a challenge I enjoyed. Being a serviceman's wife and a mother requires many skills not normally given much credit, such as prioritization, organization, planning, adaptability, handling emergencies single-handedly when the head of the household is away, etc. Over the years, as a registered nurse, teacher, and administrator, I added more skills that were useful in helping me to decide what to do upon my retirement.

Separated from my husband for several years, and finally widowed in 1996, the decision of what to do with the rest of my life was entirely in my hands.

After researching many health-related programs on the Internet, I found an article about the Peace Corps. I explored the advantages and disadvantages of becoming a volunteer in the Peace Corps. I had recently read Lillian Carter's small book about her experiences in the Peace Corps in India at the age of seventy.* Lillian did not ask for any special privileges because she was Jimmy Carter's mother. I thought, *If she can withstand the hardships of being away from her family and friends, and endure the deprivations she encountered in India, then I, too, can survive, wherever I might be assigned.*

Nevertheless, I knew my chances of being accepted into the Peace Corps were slim. I had heard stories from my friends about people who had been turned down for one reason or another. The average Peace Corps volunteer is a young person, just out of college, very idealistic, seeking adventure. However, today was a different time, and I had read that the president was encouraging older, healthy adults to join the Peace Corps.

I decided to take a gamble, and with Lillian Carter as my muse (inspiration), I applied to the Peace Corps.

* Lillian Carter and Gloria Spann Carter (1977). *Away From Home: Letters to my Family._*

Chapter Two

My Assignment

Finally, after over a year of waiting, the letter arrived with my assignment, making my acceptance into the Peace Corps official. I was assigned to Malawi, Africa. I had never heard of Malawi. When I was asked by my Peace Corps recruiter my preference for an assignment, I had answered, "Some place warm and preferably in Africa." My eventual placement in Africa at Biriwiri was one of its coldest sites. I had thought all of Africa was warm. Was I mistaken! Biriwiri was on one of the highest elevations in Malawi. I would arrive there in July, the middle of Africa's winter.

My staging orders were to fly to Washington, D.C. on June 1, 2003, to attend an orientation to the Peace Corps. After orientation, I would fly from D.C. to Amsterdam, and then to Nairobi. From Nairobi, I would fly to Lilongwe, the capital of Malawi. It would be a long flight, over 24 hours, on three different airlines. I had read the literature sent by the Peace Corps thoroughly, had passed my physical, had purchased the things on the list of recommended articles, had packed a pair of "sensible walking shoes" to take with me, and felt prepared. Some of the things that I knew I would not need right away, I packed and sent by surface mail to myself at the address given by the Peace Corps. I paid all my bills and made arrangements to have a friend stay in my town house for the next two years.

Before leaving for Washington, one final important thing I had to do was to say good-bye to my friends and family. This entailed resigning from the boards I was on, letting Planned Parenthood know I was leaving and my volunteer days with them were ending, and attending the many luncheons in my honor to say good-byes. I am certain I gained five pounds that week.

I invited my children and grandchildren to meet with me at the home of my "first born" back in Missouri by sending them the following e-mail:

April 12, 2003

Dear Ones,

This letter is to inform everyone about my plans for the next 2 ½ years. I have received my Peace Corps Assignment. I will be going to Malawi in the Southeastern part of Africa. If you have access to a map of Africa, you can look it up. I started this process over two years ago when I was getting ready to retire and was thinking about what I wanted to do with the rest of my life. At the time, all of my family was healthy and leading their own lives successfully. Since then, Holly (my granddaughter) and her husband Scott have had some medical problems following Scott's second unsuccessful kidney transplant. I spent three weeks in Missouri with them and left them thinking Scott was stable. He is now back in the hospital, in great discomfort with pericarditis. The new kidney is not working. However, they remain optimistic that it will eventually function, at least partly. Scott is back on dialysis three times a week, a treatment he was hoping to avoid.

My departure date from Colorado is May 29th. That does not give me much time to get ready. I will cancel my plans if Scott is not stable and I think Holly may need me. If he gets the pericarditis resolved and is on dialysis, there is not anything I can do for him and Holly, so I will go ahead with my plans. I can always get a leave from the Peace Corps and return in an emergency.

I hope I will have the love and support of all of you as I take this next step in my life. Let me tell you my exact plans.

I will leave Colorado on May 29th to drive to Bill's house. Maggie (my sister who lives in Pagosa Springs, Colorado) may come with me. She is still deciding if she can arrange her work. The next evening, May 30th, is a Friday and I would like for all my children to meet at Bill's house at 6:30 p.m. I will tell you all exactly what I am doing, how you can get in touch with me, what you can do for me, etc. By getting together, you will be able to ask any questions you have, and all of you will hear the information at the

9

Chapter Three

Malawi, "The Warm Heart of Africa"

Realizing that my knowledge of Africa was limited, I read everything I could find about Africa, and Malawi in particular, as I prepared to accept my assignment. Since the actress/singer Madonna, recently adopted a child in Malawi, and is in the process of building a school for Malawian girls, the country has become more newsworthy. More people have heard of Malawi.

At this time, I will share with the reader what I learned about Malawi. Remember that each country in Africa is different, and has its own government.

There are 47 countries in Africa, including the disputed territory of Western Sahara. The six islands off the coast are usually listed, making a total of 53 countries. Each country is an independent nation. The European country that colonized the country until it became independent influences how the country views itself, its language, and its customs. Describing a country in Africa is like the story of the three blind men trying to describe what an elephant is like from the part of the elephant they touched. My description cannot be applied to another country in Africa.

In my research, I soon learned that many of the names of African countries I had been taught in school had changed. Once known as Nyasaland under the British protectorate, when the country gained its independence in 1963, the name Malawi was revived. The name Malawi, meaning "Land of flaming waters" had been given to the country by the ancient Bantu empire because of the fiery sunlight reflecting on Lake Nyassa, now known as Lake Malawi.

Malawi is a mixture of religious beliefs. At the end of the 19th century, the people still believed strongly in witchcraft and held animistic world views. Remnants of these belief systems remain today in the less educated populations. The first foreign religion to reach the shores of East Central Africa was Islam, followed by Catholic missionaries for a brief period. During the last century there was a re-awaking of Islam, and a flowering of mosques built with money from Arab countries. At the same time, there was an influx of Islamic missionaries from Yemen, whose intent was to make Malawi a pivotal base from which to conquer central Africa for Islam. It was originally feared that the recent election of a Muslim, Bakili wa Muluzi, as president would further this plan. However, Muluzi continues to insist that on matters of religion he wishes to remain neutral.*

The influence of the Catholic Church has grown, as noted in the 1998 census, while the influence of

Islam has decreased. According to the 1998 census, the breakdown in Malawi was Christianity (58%), the Catholic Church (20%), Islam (12.8), other (3%) and none (4.3%).

The first significant contact with Western people began with the arrival of David Livingston, in 1859. He was a Presbyterian missionary/explorer from Scotland. While exploring the beauty of Nyasaland, Livingston discovered that it was a route for slave traders. He became an activist against this inhuman occupation, and rallied his countrymen to aid him in fighting the slave traders. He is credited with saving many Africans from being deported to America and other slave-holding countries. His influence as a missionary led to other missionaries establishing churches in Malawi.

A question asked of me by my village counterpart was whether I was a Christian. Since I am a Unitarian, I found this question difficult to answer. Realizing my answer was important to him and could impact our future working relationship, I said, "Yes, I am a Christian, but I probably do not define the term quite like you do." This seemed to satisfy him, and we worked well together.

One of the most densely populated countries in Africa, Malawi has a population of about 12 million in an area approximately the size of Indiana. It is bordered by Tanzania, Zambia, and Mozambique. When Mozambique had a civil war, in 1991, many of its citizens fled across its border into Malawi.

As a result of the influx of these people, Malawi suffered. Trees were cut down for fuel, and what was once a green, flourishing forest is now sparsely foliated in many places. Known as *The Warm Heart of Africa*, the Malawians took in their neighbors and did not turn them away.

Malawi, frequently referred to as Sub-Saharan Africa, is south of the equator, making the seasons the opposite of those in the United States. June, July, and August are the coldest months. The hottest months are October, November, and December. The rainy season starts in October or November, lasting through April. The farmers try to get their fields prepared and planted before the rainy season starts.

The geography of Malawi is dominated by a freshwater lake, Lake Malawi, which stretches down most of the eastern side of the country, covering almost one third of Malawi. The lake is a beautiful setting for many activities. The clear blue water and clean sandy beaches, bordered in places with Palm trees and resorts, reminds me of Hawaii. The lake provides a good living for fishermen, who fish mostly for Tilapia and a tasty, but bony, fish called Chamba. The lake also provides 85-90 percent of the fresh water tropical, aquarium fish in the world. When I go into Petco, or other stores that have tropical fish, I am reminded that the colorful fish they display probably came from Lake Malawi. I wondered why I did not see some of these beautiful fish in the homes as pets. Since they were freshwater fish, they would probably survive. However, I never got around to providing a space in my own house for them. Perhaps it was a matter of not having anything to feed them.

Subsistence farming is the main source of income for 95 percent of the people. The fields are readied for planting using a hoe which allows only the top soil to be turned over and prepared for seed. Corn/maize has shallow roots, making it ideal for this type of limited cultivation. Hardly any other crops are grown. Therefore, rotation of crops is not practical, and the same crop, corn, is planted each year in the same field. Growing the same crop, year after year, depletes the soil of essential nutrients, so each crop is dependent upon fertilizer being added to the soil to have a good harvest. The addition of fertilizer does not enrich the soil, but is essential for a good yield.

Fertilizer is regulated by the government and varies in cost each year, sometimes becoming so expensive that it is impossible for the farmers to afford it. The farmers are at the mercy of a greedy, unresponsive government. If a crop fails due to lack of fertilizer, the family will suffer and famine may result. The amount of rain also affects the yield at harvest time. In such times, families have been known to eat only one meal a day. The rest of the time, they limit their activities, perhaps sleeping most of the day, until the next season when things start growing again. This method of surviving may be all right for adults, but what about children who are growing and need consistent nutrition?

Nsima (finely ground field corn/maize) is the staple diet food for Malawians, just as rice or millet might be in other African countries. However, nsima is robbed of any nutrients it may contain by the method used to prepare it for cooking. Filling up on nsima, without adding protein and other foods that contain essential nutrients, leads to malnutrition, especially in children.

I will address some of the contributing factors to these community health problems in subsequent chapters.

* Taken from *Malawi: Flames in the African Sky.* Author, Luciano Nevi. (1994).

Chapter Four
Orientation in Washington D.C., and the Flight to Malawi

My roommate in D.C. was a tiny Jewish girl fresh out of college. Her name was Amanda. Her mother spent a lot of time with her, so she must have lived nearby. The group of 22 other Peace Corps recruits consisted of men and women of various ages. One newly-married couple was in the group. I obviously was the eldest. There were five nurses, a former priest, (age 60), and a young woman with dual citizenship, Irish and American. We were all classified as Community Health Volunteers. Some of the people had graduate degrees, and all had at least a Bachelors degree. The priest and I probably had the most sheepskin credentials. I wondered how much good they would do us in a third-world country.

The orientation lasted three days. We were administered at least twelve immunizations, for everything from Hepatitis B to Yellow Fever. Then we were given anti-malaria medication. I received an anti-biotic, Declocyline, as an anti-malaria medication because I was on a blood pressure medication that did not allow me to take what the other volunteers would be taking. I was not unhappy to be singled out and taking a different medication, because the side effects of taking the standard anti- malaria medication were hallucinations and frightening dreams. I was not sure I could have handled those. Once more, I decided that being older did have a few benefits. Later, because many of our classes were outside, my medication needed to be changed. I received second degree sunburn on my hands and face from the photosensitive properties of the antibiotic. The new medication, Maladrone, cost $10 a pill. I had to take a pill each day, making me a very expensive volunteer. I was warned that Maladrone was the medication of choice for the treatment of Malaria. If I became ill with Malaria, they were very vague about what medication could be used to treat me. I decided to be very faithful and compliant in taking my medication, so I would not get Malaria.

On June 3rd we were bussed to the airport. The driver got lost, and we were afraid we would miss our plane. It was raining and difficult to see the signs. After being processed at the airport, our guide tied a piece of red yarn on our suitcases so they could be easily identified at each succeeding airport. I still have the red yarn on my cases.

We left D.C. in the evening, and arrived in Amsterdam at 7:15 in the morning of the next day. There is a six hour difference in the time, so it was truly not an overnight flight. We were not scheduled to leave for Nairobi until 8:40 in the evening. In my journal I noted:

I am beginning to wonder about this adventure. The world is getting so small. Information is shared so freely. People travel so easily to various parts of the world. It seems we have saturated the world with our culture and values. How new will this group of Peace Corps people, and the information we bring, be to the Africans? I guess I will soon find out. I do not want this to be a drummed up adventure to titillate over-indulged young Americans.

Later, I made the following entry about the first stage of my flight:

This is really no fun, riding in such cramped conditions. I am in the middle seat of a five-seat row. This means I need to climb over two people either way to get to the bathroom!

After a tasty chicken dinner, I dozed and watched a movie. Maid in Manhatten. *It is now 6:30 A.M. We have just had coffee, juice, and a muffin for breakfast. It is getting light and we should be landing at Amsterdam in another hour.*

We had been told there were rooms available at the airport if anyone wanted to get a rest during the 12-hour layover in Amsterdam. I was looking forward to renting one and getting a real rest. The young couple (newlyweds) rented a room, but when I checked on the rooms I found they were all taken. Some of us wandered about the airport, but other, more adventurous members of our group, took the tram and went into town. We were warned that if we missed our connection we would be sent home. I wanted to visit The Hague, but did not think I could risk missing my flight. I had come too far to be sent home. I later learned "being sent home" was a common refrain for any infraction in the Peace Corps.

A journey entry:

I am exhausted. When we tried to get our boarding passes we were told we had to have visas. After a long wait, the airport personnel contacted the embassy in Malawi. They had to wait until 11 A.M. to call the embassy due to the time difference. Since the small hotel in the airport was filled, I wandered around the airport, visiting the shops, and then went to the Meditation Lounge which had lounge type chairs with a continuous viewing screen of nature scenes from Holland. It was not like lying on a bed, but I did get a little rest.

We left Amsterdam on a Boeing 767, a new Kenya Airways plane. There was more room, and it was more comfortable. Everything was new and modernized. Each seat had a tiny T.V. on the back of the seat ahead. There were only 3 seats in the middle instead of five like yesterday. The T.V. included a sign interpreter for deaf passengers.

The flight to Nairobi, Kenya, another all-night flight, arrived in Nairobi at 6:10 in the morning. As we landed, I looked out the window and saw on the horizon a panorama of black, flat Acadia trees silhouetted against the orange streaks of the dawn. *Just like a photo in National Geographic*, I thought. With this picture came the realization that I was truly in Africa!

The last leg of our flight was a short one of 3 hours and 40 minutes, ending in Lilongwe, the capital of Malawi, at 11:49 in the morning. I had changed into a dress in Nairobi, so I would be dressed conservatively out of respect for the culture, remembering that first impressions are so important. When we finally landed, we all cheered. We were exhausted. My hips ached from walking and standing on concrete for twelve hours in the Amsterdam airport.

I was glad to be back on terra firma safely, and in Malawi at last.

Chapter Five
My First Day in Malawi

We debarked from the plane, and passed through customs. A group of Peace Corps volunteers and Peace Corps officials were waiting to greet us. A woman stepped forward from the crowd and introduced herself to me saying, "I am Mary Ann. Until now, I was the oldest volunteer here in Malawi." I knew then that our applications and profiles had been forwarded to the Peace Corps office and had been reviewed by the current group of volunteers! Mary Ann had flaming red hair and the kindest face. I knew immediately that I had found a friend in my new country.

Leaving the welcoming group, we boarded a bus which held exactly 24 people. Our luggage was placed in two Land Rovers emblazoned with the Peace Corps logo. We were transported to the Dedza School of Forestry, a two hour drive from Lilongwe. As we drove along there were people everywhere, sitting by the road, walking with bundles on their heads, riding bicycles, etc. I saw thatched homes, women pounding nsima (maize/corn) in huge wooden mortars with wooden pestles, vendors selling roasted corn, fruit, and vegetables. They held up their wares to the windows of the bus. We were not able to buy anything, because we did not have any legal tender, kwacha. There were oxcarts hauling loads of neatly stack rows of corn. The sights, sounds, and smells were strange and exciting. Many of the activities I was witnessing I had only read about until now.

Leaving the main highway, the MI, we turned onto a dirt road. The road was rough. It did not look that rocky, but we bounced along as if the bus had no springs. Up to then, I had never experienced a more bumpy, teeth-jarring ride. I thought for certain we would break an axle. This ride remains in my memory, but it was certainly not to be my last such ride. Only the main highway, the MI, is paved in Malawi.

By now it was getting dusk in the thick trees lining each side of the road. The headlights picked up my first sight of wild animals, as a pack of baboons crossed the road headed for trees to nest in for the night, after raiding a nearby cornfield. A huge male baboon paused in front of the slowed bus to show his fangs as he leered at us defiantly. I hoped I would not meet him in daylight. He looked very fierce.

When we arrived at the Forestry School, we were greeted by our new teachers. All of them were Malawians and spoke excellent English. Most had been educated in Great Britain, I learned later. They welcomed us with a song of greeting and a traditional dance. Tired as we were, we quickly became infected with their enthusiasm, and soon we were all dancing with them.

When the welcoming ceremony was over, we were assigned a double room in the school dormitory. I had a feeling of "déjà vu" when I entered my rustic room. I felt as if I had been here before. Perhaps it reminded me of the rooms at Ghost Ranch in New Mexico, where I spent a week retreat with my church one summer. Each bed had a blue mosquito net over the bed. On the night table beside the twin bed, neatly laid out, were 3 bars of soap, a candle, matches, a map of Malawi, 3 lined notebooks, an eraser, a pencil, and a pen. There were also two airmail envelopes with enough Malawi stamps for mailing letters home, and a bottle of water. The bed had thin, faded, gaudy printed sheets, and a thick, dark, rough, plaid wool blanket. The floor was smooth, worn concrete. The windows had metal frames with no screens.

After settling in our rooms, we were escorted to the Dining Hall, in a separate building, for "tea." Tea consisted of instant cocoa, tea, coffee, and an orange drink somewhat like Tang. Milk was in a pint bottle, more like cream. There was natural peanut butter, honey, and jam to put on whole wheat bread sliced into thick slabs. Biscuits (cookies to you and me) were also served.

Still in a slight daze from our new surroundings and perhaps a bit of 'jet lag', we were escorted to another building to attend a "Cultural Fair."

Four different stations were set up in classrooms, displaying: Nutrition, Home Stay, Culture Literature, and Health Care. A teacher was positioned at each station to explain the display, give a demonstration if appropriate, and answer questions.

The Home Stay station showed how nsima was cooked over an open fire with an iron pot balanced on three rocks. Nsima is field corn that has been finely ground into flour. It is then cooked to a thick paste. It is eaten by rolling a piece the size of a marshmallow into a ball and dipped into a relish (ndiwo) made of tomatoes, onions, and beans or greens, then popped into the mouth. I had read about this dish and was anxious to taste it. I liked corn grits when I lived in Alabama, and I liked corn mush and cornbread when I was growing up in Missouri. I was looking forward to enjoying nsima.

The Nutrition station had examples of the foodstuffs that are available in Malawi. Nearly every kind of vegetable is grown in Malawi. Tomatoes, potatoes, cabbage, beans, sweet potatoes, and cooked pumpkin seem to be the most popular. Mangoes and bananas are the most available fruit.

The Cultural Literature booth had books on teaching projects. I borrowed one on *Orphans, Barriers to Health Behavior Change in Malawi.* I had read about the numerous orphans in Malawi. An orphan, I learned, was classified as a child under the age of eighteen whose parents, either one or both, had died, usually from Malaria, Tuberculosis (TB), or HIV/AIDs. Many orphans did not have relatives to care for them. I learned that some people, even extended family, who took in orphans, used them as slaves, depriving them of an education. Others did their best to care for and feed the extra mouths in spite of their limited resources.

The Health booth informed us about the common health problems, HIV being the most prevalent. The need for clean water and sanitation was stressed. These topics became the primary focus of the following training sessions. We learned the importance of hand washing after using the chimbudzi (toilet) because of the prevalence of hepatitis. Something as simple as draining dishes after they were washed was a health problem for some homes.

At 6:30, we returned to the dining room for supper. The Nationals (workers and students at the school) had a huge plate of nsima which they ate with their fingers. When we Peace Corps Trainees (PCT) were served, the nsima had been replaced with rice, and silverware was supplied. I was so disappointed. I was prepared to eat nsima; had in fact been looking forward to eating it! A salad had been made just for us. The rest of the meal consisted of greens, peas, and stewed chicken, or was it goat or beef? I never decided what it was. It was stewed to be indistinguishable, but delicious. We had more of the wonderful brown bread. We served ourselves water from large water filter dispensers. We had been warned not to drink water that had not been boiled and filtered. Dessert was fresh fruit, bananas, and mangos.

After supper, I took a hot shower, washed the dust out of my hair, and climbed into my bed. I arranged the mosquito net around me, tucking it carefully under the mattress, and crashed at about 8:30 p.m.

We were awakened at 5:30 A.M. Breakfast was served at 6:30. Breakfast was delicious. It consisted of hot oatmeal called "Jungle Oats," served with bottled cream, which was probably irradiated because it was kept on a shelf until it was opened. Fried eggs and more of the thick, brown bread completed the breakfast. I had hot tea with sugar. Tea is grown in Malawi. The best is exported, but what I had was delicious

In my journal I noted:

The people here really are as nice and warm as they have been portrayed to be. They are always laughing or dancing to any music they hear, tympanically or in their hearts.

I guess this is why Malawi is called "The Warm Heart of Africa."

Chapter Six
Getting Down to Business

After breakfast the next day, we began our first day of training with a review of our health histories and two more immunizations, tetanus and meningitis. In my journal I noted my appreciation for how we were being treated:

> *I have lost count of the immunizations I have had. At least they are spreading them out so that we do not get them all in one day.*

On our first day of Orientation we gathered in a classroom where Wellington, a neatly dressed Malawian, who was in charge of our training, talked to us about the schedule for our training. He told us we will practice riding on the Mini-buses and will visit our assigned village where we will be doing five weeks of "home stay." I was leery about riding on the buses, especially by myself. Everyone piles on them with their "katundu" (shopping bags and paraphernalia), chickens, goats, children and whatever they are transporting. The buses can get very crowded. Would I be able to get off at my site? I was not looking forward to this new experience.

In the afternoon, a banker came and took our American money into town to deposit it into a bank. He gave each Peace Corps Trainee (PCT) $140 in Kwacha, Malawian currency, for "walking about money." "Walking about money" was a new term for me, but I would hear it again and again! It meant money for incidental expenses such as bus fare.

We were issued our First Aid Kits by the Doctor. The kits were the size of brief cases. The doctor went over everything in the kit with us. She went into great detail as she told us how to draw our own blood if we got malaria. I wondered how many people before me had had to do that? It sounded unrealistic if you were chilling and really ill to be able to find a vein, draw the blood and put it into the proper container. I resolved to take my anti-malaria medication faithfully so I would never get malaria. After that we were issued three books; *Where There is No Cook, Where There is No Doctor, and Staying Healthy in Malawi.* Being a visual learner, I love to read. I could hardly wait to get back to my room and start reading.

For the next several weeks we attended classes, always stopping around 4 p.m. for tea. I looked forward to this break from classes. We learned about the culture, and began learning the native language, Chichewa. The teachers were so patient. They wanted us to learn everything we would need to survive. They used a variety of teaching techniques such as role playing and humor. I developed a great respect for their knowledge and teaching methods. One teacher in particular became our favorite. He always started his class with a "hokey" joke. For example:

"A man was driving along when his car broke down. It was a long way to a town either way. He decided to take the car apart and walk back to the nearest town carrying the part. He took a door off and was walking along carrying it on his head. The day was hot and dusty. He met a man who asked him what he was doing. After hearing the first man's explanation, the man said, "But aren't you very hot?" "Oh, it is not too bad," the first man replied, "I have the window rolled down."

I noted in my journal:

We are learning so much I do not know if I can keep it all in my head. I am having trouble learning the language. Probably because I am older and not bilingual. Learning a new language is usually easier for the young ones.

Sometimes the classes were held outside. Guest speakers, such as more seasoned PCV's, talked to us about their experiences. I was in awe over the stories they told us. It was all so new and exciting. I looked forward to being like them, a PC Volunteer (PCV), no longer a PC Trainee (PCT). This transition would not happen until we had finished our home stay at the end of our training and had been "sworn in" by the American Ambassador at the Embassy in Lilongwe.

Every day we checked in the office to see if we had received a letter from home. Letters were so welcome. I felt so disconnected from the world, but never homesick. During this part of our training there were no computers available to check our e-mail unless we could hitch a ride with one of the drivers back to Lilongwe to the Peace Corps office.

Some of the younger PCT's soon discovered a "bottle store" nearby. A bottle store is like a bar. After classes, in the evening, several PCT's would disappear to have a few beers, listen to music and perhaps dance. Wellington invited the trainees to his home which was nearby, where more partying happened. One young woman spent the night sleeping on the grass because she could not find her way back to the dormitory or was too drunk to care. I was shocked when I learned of this and thought about the dangers she had exposed herself to such as snakes. As an older trainee, I did not join the parties, but understood the younger crowd were transitioning from college parties to adjusting to life in a foreign land. I wished they would be careful but I did not want to fulfill the "mother" role. Only once did I feel the need to chastise a young man for doing something I felt was inappropriate, and insulting to our hosts. I reminded him his actions reflected poorly on all of us. He had "mooned" our

Land Rover when he was riding in a Land Rover in front of us. To me it was a sophomoric, crude, type of humor common in America, a daring sport there, but showing body parts was considered offensive in Africa. I could tell our Malawian driver was offended, but he did not say anything. I was embarrassed for him. I am sure he was very confused when everyone laughed and did not understand what was so funny. Malawians like their homemade beer and enjoy a good joke as much as anyone. But, exposing your body by "mooning" someone was beyond his comprehension.

At the end of our stay in the comfortable dormitories we were divided into three groups. Each group was sent to a different village to spend five weeks in "home stay." Home stay meant we would each live with a Malawian family for the remaining five weeks of our orientation. The average Malawian family lived in a small mud hut with a thatched roof. The huts were unheated, dark, with cramped living quarters which were sometimes shared at night with chickens, goats, and perhaps , even a pig. The animals were brought inside for protection from hyenas who scavenged the village dumps at night.

It was July, the coldest month of the year in Malawi.

I was not looking forward to home stay!

Chapter Seven

Home Stay and My Hospital Stay

My group of seven PCTs loaded our luggage, along with our foam mattresses and woolen blankets from the dormitory at the Dedza Forestry College onto the top of one of the Peace Corps Land Rovers. Looking like traveling nomads, we were taken to our next assignment, a village called Malanda, for our five week stint of "home stay". This experience, near the end of our training period, was to give us a realistic taste of how the average Malawian lived.

On the way we stopped in Dedza, a small town with a few shops, to purchase things we would need during home stay. At the Forestry College we were allowed to wear blue jeans but such attire was a "no, no" when we were off campus.

The women in our group bought brightly colored chitenje's, a sarong type of skirt, worn by the women in Malawi. Hilary, our young vibrant Irish/American PCT bought a bright pink patterned chitenje. Nearly everything she owned was pink. In class one day her chitenje fell off to reveal her only piece of clothing that was not pink. It was a bright red petticoat. She was so embarrassed. Somehow, we Americans had trouble wrapping a chitenje around our body and keeping it in place.

My Malawians friends told me I looked pregnant in my chitenje.

I bought a covered plastic bowl to use as a potty so I wouldn't have to go out to the chimbudzi (toilet) in the dark at night. My roommate, Carol, at the Forestry College had fallen trying to make this trip in the dark. She had to be sent back to the states for a year to recuperate from her injuries. Carol had just returned to finish her commitment to the Peace Corps. I was glad she had warned me of this hazard.

A flashlight, a terry cloth towel and washcloth, and several rolls of pink toilet paper completed my purchases. The pink toilet paper reminded me of my travels in China. In Beijing, a man sat outside the toilet and dispensed two sheets of pink toilet paper to each person entering the toilet. This cultural quirk amused me. However, in Malawi we PCVs quickly found that most Malawians did not use toilet paper at all! Therefore, we carried toilet paper in our pockets or backpack wherever we went. To forget or run out of toilet paper was tantamount to a disaster for the fastidious among us.

Malanda is a small village in the Ntcheu district. It consisted of small mud huts with thatched roofs. It was about two miles or four kilometers from the MI. The MI was the principal paved road in Malawi, stretching from one end of the country to the other. I think the term MI stood for Malawi

Interstate. There was a Health Centre, a church and several schools. There were no buses that came to the village regularly. If you wanted to go into Lilongwe, the state capital and headquarters for the Peace Corps, or any other place, you had to walk or cycle to the MI and catch a bus there.

Malanda was the site where Mary Ann, the woman I met at the airport, was assigned. She had lived there for a year. She was a fountain of knowledge concerning the Peace Corps and life in a different culture. She had already been in Africa for two years at another site in Lethosoto. It was obvious she loved Africa and its people and they loved her, especially the children. The numerous projects she started with support from her friends back in the states were appreciated by the village.

Mary Ann started a pre-school and helped in the Health Centre by making curtains for the Maternity Unit and the children's unit. She supervised painting and decorating the drab walls. She made a library in a large room next to the school. The entire wall of one side of the room was painted with a colorful map of Africa by a talented Malawian artist.

Mary Ann extended her tour in Malanda for a year in order to finish some of the programs she had started, then transferred to Botswana and completed another two year tour. She became the "poster " volunteer for the Peace Corps. She is featured in many of the Peace Corps brochures and video's. A registered nurse with a Master's degree she is a role model for the older volunteer.

Arriving in Malanda our new host amayi (women/mothers) were waiting for us. A tall young woman stepped forward to greet me. Her name she said was Madalo. She said I would be staying in her house with her mother and son for the next five weeks. She then picked up my mattress and balancing it on her head she picked up my suitcase and headed for her house. Astounded at her ability to carry so much with ease, I trailed behind her carrying the rest of my essentials.

When we reached her house, which was surrounded by a grass fence forming a courtyard of sorts, she sat down her load and opened the door. Linly, Madalo's mother and Tendai, Madalo's ten-year-old son, were waiting to greet us. I gasped as I stepped over the threshold to her house and blurted out, "It is beautiful!" The modest one room was neat and tidy. The floor was dirt but hard as cement and swept clean. A few wicker chairs and a small wicker divan were adorned with freshly laundered, yellow, embroidered doilies. A large wooden Chief's chair, the type that is found in many Pier One stores in the states, sat regally in one corner. On a wooden coffee table stood a bouquet of yellow asters in a green brandy bottle. A pot of tea with cups and sugar was ready to welcome their new boarder, me.

Linly's home where the author stayed during home-stay

Linly, smiled shyly, apparently pleased at my enthusiastic outburst. I learned later that Linly was my age, 74. I was amazed. In my research about Malawi I had read that the average life span was around 38-40. I decided Linly grew up and had her family of eight, alive, and healthy children before the pandemic of AIDs. An older person in Malawi is highly respected and addressed as an "agogo." The A is a term of respect. Gogo means an older person.

Madalo placed my mattress in a second room on a small wooden bed. I realized this must have been Linly's room. Apparently she slept in the bed without a mattress. A small wooden desk and a chair stood in one corner. I looked at the thatched roof and wondered if it contained lizards or bugs or even mice. It did not disclose any vermin during my stay as Linly was a proud housekeeper. I was very lucky and appreciated my upgraded surroundings. I learned I was the third PCT Madalo had hosted. The first one was a man, the second one was Mary Ann, who now had her own house not far away in Malanda.

After settling into my room, I went outside and sat down on the veranda beside Linly who was shelling maize (corn). I picked up an ear and started helping her. I do not remember Linly speaking much English and I was just beginning to learn Chichewa, but we had no trouble communicating. Madalo was able to speak a little more English. I learned that Madalo was the teacher at a pre-school started by Mary Ann.

When it was time to eat, I went inside. Madalo brought a bowl and a pitcher of water. She poured the water over my hands and handed me a small towel. She then performed the same ritual for her mother and Tendai. It was a ritual carried out in every Malawian home before eating. It seemed almost Biblical in nature, reminding me of the washing of feet by Jesus in the New Testament.

Madalo brought me a plate filled with rice and a relish of beans, onions, and tomatoes. I was so thankful that Madalo did not expect me to cook for myself. She gave me a spoon which I realized was probably the only one she had. The rest of the family ate with their fingers. My first meal in my new home was delicious and I was famished.

After eating, neighbors and extended family gathered in the small room curious to meet the new PCT. Most of the people sat on the floor. One young girl, a teenager or perhaps in her early twenties, seemed unwelcome. I noticed how a woman tried to get her to leave the room. I said, "No, let her stay." I learned later she was epileptic and considered mentally deficient. Her name was Miriam. She did not talk much but I soon found she was a good worker. Her family seemed to be ashamed of her and hadn't allowed her to attend school. I thought to myself, if she was in America she could have had medication that would have controlled her seizures and allowed her to live a more productive, normal life. Miriam's family probably considered her possessed, especially when she had a seizure.

As time passed during my home stay I remained friendly toward Miriam and she reciprocated by running to meet me as I returned from school and insisted upon carrying my bundles home for me. I had the feeling she watched for my return each day.

Having a PCT stay with you was considered an honor. It elevated the family's standing within the community. The host family did not receive any monetary compensation. They did get food rations ever so often delivered by the Peace Corps Home Stay Coordinator, Christine, consisting of a chicken, eggs, bread, tea, rice and sugar. Some of the PCTs complained that they never did get served any of the chicken. I guess the host families ate it.

My peers in Malanda did not fare as well as I. I think I had the best housing of any one. Perhaps it was because of my age or I was just lucky. It never occurred to me at anytime to ask for any special consideration because of my age. I wanted to be treated the same as any other PCT. My age was my problem. Most of my peers slept on the floor on a woven reed mat. One complained about the mice that ran over her in the night. Another woke to find a large black tarantula on her mosquito net. The gecko's chattered all night and ran across the ceiling. They were welcomed in the houses because they helped to keep the cockroach and bug problem under control. I learned to tune them out.

Linly slept on the floor in front of my bedroom door. It was like having a guard outside my door. I could hear her reading her Bible before she went to sleep. I felt safe and secure as I listened to the night sounds which were so different in Africa. The dogs would bark and the hyenas would howl an echo. It reminded me of the coyotes and wolves in Colorado. Linly would not allow me to get up in the morning until she had rolled up her reed mat and swept the dirt floor. Madalo and Tendia slept in a separate hut which also served as a store room. Since there were no closets in the huts, extra clothes etc. were kept in old suitcases. This kept them clean and away from rodents.

Madalo arose at 5:30 every morning to walk the half mile to the bore hole, in the center of the village. There she would stand in line to draw water, while chatting with her neighbors until her turn. Balancing her water container on her head she would come home to cook breakfast for her mother, son and me. For breakfast she would serve eggs, bread, if she had it, or porridge (phala) and hot tea. She was so thoughtful, she even made a snack for me to take with me when I went to my language classes. The snack might consist of peanuts (ground nuts/mtedza), a banana (nthochi) or cold sweet potato (mbatata). All of the food was cooked over a small charcoal stove. Sometimes she cooked over a wood fire made by balancing a pot on three rocks. Pulling the sticks in and out of the flame adjusted the heat. Not being a picky eater, I enjoyed every morsel she gave me. I wondered how some of my more finicky, younger, peers were faring?

One evening I could hear a moaning noise made by some kind of an animal a few huts away. Another PCT, John, who apparently lived close to the family that had the animal, said it was a goat (mbuzi) that was ill and dying. The moaning continued off and on all night. The next day as I was going to class I could no longer hear the suffering animal, I presumed it had died. That evening Madalo served me goat meat in my relish. I knew it probably came from the dead goat, but I ate it anyway. Protein was a scarce commodity in Malawi. I am sure the goat was butchered and shared with many families in the village. Since there is no refrigeration, any meat that is obtained has to be used immediately. I crossed my fingers and hoped the goat did not die from some fatal, perhaps contagious, illness.

Madalo's kitchen was a separate mud hut. Bags of corn were stored in the kitchen. On one bag of corn sat a speckled hen on a nest of eggs soon to be hatched. Very few small chicks survived because of the chicken hawks who would swoop down and snatched a fluffy chick for a juicy meal. When the mother hen saw a shadow on the ground she would cluck for her chicks to come and they all ran under a bush until the frightening shadow was gone. On one side of the kitchen was a small shed that housed the few goats Madalo owned. The goats roamed the village during the day, returning at night to be locked in the shed.

My laundry was taken care of by Miriam, usually while I was at school. One day I came home to find her washing my Jean's jacket by pounding it on a rock with a second rock. When Miriam was finished with my jacket, it was truly "stone washed" and a lighter blue then the original navy blue! I complimented her for doing such a good job.

I still wear that jacket and think of Miriam and the thorough trouncing she gave it using rocks!

I was well cared for by Linly and Madalo except for one thing. It was July, the coldest month of the year and I was always cold, even in my bed at night with blankets and my coat on my bed, and wearing my clothes. Occasionally Linly would light the charcoal stove to add additional heat to warm the room. I knew this was costing her money, but I truly appreciated it. I was so cold I had difficulty focusing on my language lessons.

Every day I walked about half a mile, past the borehole where Madalo drew water, to attend classes held in a cold building, to try to learn Chechewa, the native language. I think the teachers thought we were a bunch of pansies because we all complained of the cold. I can not learn when my teeth are chattering so much I can hardly pronounce the words. The teachers made hot tea for us and that helped a little.

One day the teachers ran out of tea. I invited all seven PCTs home and asked Linly to make us hot tea. Always the gracious hostess, she smiled at my impetuous request. She warmly welcomed my friends and shook hands with each of them then left the room. In a few minutes, as if my magic, she had tea ready for us. Later I thought about my empirical request and realized I should have asked if she had enough tea and enough cups to serve all of us. Or did she even have enough fire wood to heat water for tea? I had treated her like a servant. But Linly did not seem to mind and forgave me. We all were so grateful for her kindness.

I could hardly wait for the five weeks of home stay to be over. I have never been so cold in my life. I felt as if the cold had gone clear into my bones. Perhaps it was because I was older and did not have a layer of fat to keep me warm that I suffered from the cold. I thought about the winters on the farm where I grew up. The snow would be over the fence tops and lay in huge drifts. I did not mind the cold then. But of course I could always return to a warm house to thaw out after being outside. None of the huts in Malawi had any source of heat. It was as if the people were used to the cold and just adapted to the weather, waiting patiently until the warmer weather returned. However, I could not seem to adapt. I stumbled as I walked to my classes every day. I could hardly wait for classes to be over so I could hurry home to crawl into my bed and try to get warm.

Madalo pampered me by placing a tub in my room and pouring hot water into it every evening for my bath. The rest of the family bathed in the bath house outside. The bath house consisted of a small shed of mud with rocks for the floor and a thatched roof. The bather took an "elephant" bath. They soaped their body then poured water over their body using a large cup. Then, wrapped in an old chitenje, they hurried into the house to finish dressing. I was thankful that Madalo was so thoughtful in providing a bath tub for me inside. The bath house usually contained spiders and cobwebs and of course no light. If it was dark there might also be a snake resting in it. Malawians take one or two baths a day. Sometimes I wanted to skip my bath and go straight to bed, but I knew this would be offensive to my hosts so I bathed religiously every night. The attention to cleanliness was important to remove the dust and keep down any skin diseases.

Linly, Madalo, Tendai with two male cousins

The toilet or "chimbudzi" was also outside. It consisted of a building similar to the bath house except it had a cement floor with an opening in the floor over which you squatted. Again , it harbored spiders and an occasional snake. I did not like using the chimbudzi, especially at night, so I used the plastic bowl I had purchased as a chamber pot. It had a lid on it and I emptied it myself every morning into the chimbudzi. Malawians do not use toilet paper and I was always forgetting to take some with me when I had to use the chimbudzi. A roll of pink toilet paper quickly became standard equipment for all PCT's back packs. One PCT, Mary, dropped her wallet into the chimbudzi. It had all of her money in it and fell out of her pocket when she stooped over. The pit is 30 feet deep so there was no way to retrieve it. I felt sorry for Mary, but at the time I was feeling so sorry for myself that it was all I could do to keep myself going without worrying about what happened to someone else.

Part of our training was to teach the villagers to wash their hands after going to the chimbudzi. Hepatitis was rampant in the villages and hand washing was important. Madalo had a hand washing device beside her chimbudzi. It consisted of a forked tree limb embedded in the ground. A plastic jug of water hung on one fork of the limb. A plastic lid was balanced in the center of the fork. On the lid was a bar of soap covered with a leaf so the birds would not eat it. Ashes could also be used if soap was not available. When a person left the chimbudzi there was no excuse for him/her not to wash their hands. Madalo took advantage of everything that was taught by the PCTs. Having had three PCTs live with her she was very observant and put into practice everything she learned from them.

Teacher demonstrating a hand washing device

Every day we walked to the language classes held in a cold unheated house with the window panes broken and wind whistling through the cracks in the door. I was unable to learn a new language when I was so cold and miserable.

Our teachers lived in the house and cooked their meals outside. They were sympathetic to our complaints of being cold. Besides making hot tea for us, another strategy to warm us up was to have us go outside into the sun and do jumping jacks or other exercises to get the circulation going. I resisted these maneuvers psychologically. I just wanted to be warm. I realized it would do no good to complain after witnessing how one of my peers, was treated.

We were sitting in an open veranda, in the cold air, on the cold cement benches patients sat on as they waited for treatment in a clinic. The teacher was talking about how drama or outdoor theater was used to teach the illiterate population we would be encountering about AIDs and HIV. He had asked a drama group located in the village to give us a demonstration of a skit they had composed. Sarah, a young PCT, interrupted the teacher and asked to be taken to the health clinic at the Peace Corps Office because she could not breathe. She was having an asthma attack.

The teacher was so engrossed in what he was showing us that he asked her to wait until the demonstration was finished or perhaps she could wait until the next day to go to the health clinic. Being a nurse, I was very concerned that the girl would pass out and go into respiratory arrest. She did not have her inhalator with her and was going into acute distress. Most people with chronic asthma know their own bodies and how they need to be treated. Because she was still sitting upright and had not turned purple, I guess the teacher did not think she was in any really acute distress! Fortunately a PC Land Rover was available and she was transported to the health clinic still an hour away, but in time to get the proper treatment for her.

Realizing I had not brought enough heavy clothing to be properly dressed for the cold weather, I piled on every sweater and jacket I had. I looked like a bag lady. Malawians never knew or cared about the temperature. They seemed to have two seasons, cold and rainy. Whatever the day brought was just, "God's will." I never saw a thermometer anywhere. However, I was determined to stick it out and made it, but by the time the classes were over I was very ill. When I walked the short distance to the classroom each morning, past the community bore hole, I staggered like a drunken person as I walked. I had developed a productive cough. I counted the days when this ordeal would be over. Once I thought we were on the last week when I discovered we had one more week to complete this assignment. I was truly depressed.

One bright spot in the middle of this "trial of torture" was a surprise birthday party for me. Kathy, an older volunteer, told me Mary Ann wanted us to come to her house for supper in the evening. I was so happy to do something different and appreciated Mary Ann's thoughtfulness. I told Madalo I would not be home for the evening meal. Kathy came by to walk with me to Mary Ann's house. I had never been in another house in Malanda and was eager to see how a real PCV, one who was no longer a PCT, lived and survived in Malawi. Kathy and I had become good friends. Being a nurse, she was sensitive to my physical discomfort and had sympathized with me when I discovered we had another week of home stay and cold classrooms to endure.

Arriving at Mary Ann's I heard voices in the house. I said to Kathy, "Is Mary Ann expecting other guests besides us?" Kathy did not answer me. Instead she opened the door. Inside the house were the rest of our group of seven, a teacher and Mary Ann. They all shouted, "Surprise." I was stunned, then realized this secret party was in honor of my 75th birthday. I felt so honored. In my misery and feeling so sorry for myself I had completely forgotten about my birthday!

Mary Ann had decorated her house with balloons and had prepared a delicious meal of spaghetti, deviled eggs and relishes, that reminded everyone of food found in America. We ate until we were stuffed. For dessert she had made a pudding and fruit layered in tall glasses. I was so full I could not eat mine. I often thought about that dessert I had turned down. It looked so inviting. Mary Ann had a freezer in which she could keep some foods cold as long as the electricity was working, which was sporadic. I do not know where she got this electrical appliance. It probably had been handed down from one owner to the next until Mary Ann was the lucky inheritor. No one else, PCTs or PCVs that is, had such a luxury.

After eating, Mary Ann had arranged games for us to play. We played pin the tail on the donkey only the donkey was a boat and the tail was a fish on the boater's hook. Then we played spin the bottle with the person who became "it" having to tell a story and the others guessed if it was true. I told a wild yarn that had everyone feeling sorry for me until I said it was a hoax. We laughed and for awhile the trials we were all going through faded into the background and were temporarily forgotten.

My 75th birthday party at Mary Ann's house. Left to right, Noel, Kathy, the author, John, Sarah, Hilary

At the end of our home stay, we were told we needed to thank the Chief and the headmen in the village for allowing us to use their village as a training site, opening their home to us during home stay etc. I had been forewarned of this custom by a returned PCV, Tamara, who had been assigned to Malawi previously. She told me how important it was to keep communication open with the Chiefs and show them respect. She suggested I take a present to give to the Chief. I had brought with me a baseball cap gaudily decorated in gold embroidery, with American motifs, (an eagle, the flag, U.S.A. etc.) specifically for this occasion.

On the designated day, we were all escorted to the Chief's home at the far end of the village. We sat on reed mats on the ground and waited for the Chief's appearance. In our five weeks in the village none of us had ever met the Chief. I expected him to live in a home far superior to the villagers, one fit for a Chief. I looked around from my position sitting on the ground, and surveyed the run-down looking mud hut before me. Several raggedy children were running around the area, stopping to stare at us. Why were they not in school? A young woman with a baby appeared and sat down. Someone whispered to me that the children were the Chief's progeny and the young woman was <u>one</u> of the Chief's wives.

A gaunt looking old man dressed in what appeared to be rags, came out of the hut and sat down facing us. Was this the Chief? I could not believe my eyes.

With our teachers prompting us, we managed to say a few words to the old man in Chichewa. I gave him the cap and he smiled his thanks. We all said, "Zikomo kambiri" (Thank you very much) and rose to leave, our duty finished and the protocol completed. I had a hard time wrapping my American mind around the fact that the Chief appeared to be the poorest man in the village, living by ancient customs with more than one wife!

When the Land Rover came to pick us up to take us into Lilongwe for the swearing in ceremony at the Embassy where we would all become PCVs (Peace Corps Volunteers) no longer PCTs (Peace Corps Trainees), I went instead to the Peace Corps Health Clinic where I was diagnosed with pneumonia and a "fulminating " bladder infection, as Shelia, the P.A. (Physician's Assistant) described my urine, which was the color of tea, concentrated from lack of fluids and full of red blood cells. I had not even noticed. I was too cold to feel my body.

Shelia, who had been a registered nurse prior to becoming a Physician's Assistant, gave me a breathing treatment, piled blankets on me and put a warm hot water bottle on my spasming bladder. As I stopped shivering and was able to breathe better, I thought to myself, "Thank goodness the P.A. had been a nurse. What doctor would think of such comfort measures as a "hot water bottle?" Evelyn, the nurse, made hot tea for me and slowly I started to revive. I was going to make it! The tortuous ordeal of home stay and cold class rooms was over. Now, I needed to get well enough to face the next test, living on my own in a new village.

Still needing some time to recuperate, I was taken to a small British clinic where I stayed for several days. I missed the swearing in ceremony at the Embassy. This very important, formal ritual celebrates the closing of the training period as the trainees take an oath to become full fledged Peace Corps Volunteers (PCVs).

It was tradition for the Peace Corps to transport the Malawian hosts from home stay to the ceremony. This was a treat for the host families. They seldom were able to go into the big city of Lilongwe, which was two hours away by minibus for most of the families. Linly had given me a new chitenji to wear to the swearing in. I was so touched by her gift. She had carefully hemmed it by hand. It was black with a yellow pattern. I was so disappointed that I was not able to wear it to the swearing in ceremony. I had given Madalo and Linly K500 each in case they needed money for something. It was the least I could do in my limited circumstances, sick in a hospital.

Another tradition was to give a gift to the amayi and her family for taking care of us during home stay. My good friend, Kathy, came to my rescue. She made a photo album of pictures I had taken of Madalo and her family for me to give to them. I was so pleased with her idea and in her debt since I was too ill to take care of this tradition myself. I had truly appreciated the care Madalo and Linly had lavished on me so unselfishly.

I noted in my journal:

Christine, the P.C. home stay supervisor, brought Madalo, Linley, and Mary Ann to see me in the hospital. Christine is so thoughtful and kind. She wanted me to give Madalo and Linley, their certificates for being my host family. She took a picture of us which will probably be added to the photo album. They brought me some of the goodies that had been served at the ceremony. I was too ill to eat them. I gave them to the nursing staff. I gave the photo book to Madalo and Linley and thanked them for taking care of me.

When my friends left, I lay in my bed and wondered what my peers were doing? I knew it would be a long time before I saw any of them again. I wondered how the swearing in ceremony went? Wellington had told me he would take me to the Embassy when I was well for a swearing in ceremony just for me. I appreciated his thoughtfulness. However, I regretted missing such an important occasion. I knew it was a once in a lifetime event and I had missed it!.

As I slowly regained my strength, I was pleasantly surprised at the treatment I received in the hospital. I think I was the only patient in the little modern British hospital. Lying in bed, feeling sorry for myself, with nothing to read, no radio or TV, yet too ill to enjoy those things if they had been available, I heard a tap at my door and in came an aide bringing a tray of hot English tea. I love hot tea and certainly needed the liquids. This thoughtful routine of serving tea to patients reminded me that Malawi was once colonized by the British. Serving tea twice a day was a hold over of a British tradition. Sometimes there would be a small biscuit or two on the tray. I looked forward to these repasts. I knew I was not completely forgotten, although my peers did not know where I was and would have been unable to visit me anyway; they were all at their new sites busy adjusting to whatever they found there.

There was a bathroom in my suite with a tub. A real tub! I could not believe my good luck. I had been thinking, if only I could get warm again I would feel better. I ran the hot water in the tub and soaked in it several times until the heat went clear to my cold bones. I have never been so cold in my life.

Shelia visited me faithfully every day until she had to leave Malawi to attend a Seminar in Washington, D.C. A doctor took Shelia's place. He checked my lungs then ordered an x-ray and changed my antibiotic to a broad spectrum one, cephlaphin. Evidently the zithromax was not working.

As I slowly felt more like myself and an x-ray showed my lungs to be clear, I explored my surroundings by sitting in the doorway to the garden outside and enjoyed the singing of the birds and the neatly trimmed lawn. A gardenia bush grew by the door. A Poinsettia tree flowered in one corner of the garden. I had heard Poinsettia's grew large in California but in Malawi they were actual trees with plate sized blossoms.

When I was sufficiently recovered, I was taken first to the Korean Lodge to continue my recuperation for two more days then to the transit house. Laura, another PCV, was staying in the transit house. She had been ill with vomiting. We were the only guests in the transit house. Everyone else had been transported to their assigned sites.

Wellington came to take me to the Embassy to be sworn in. He was accompanied by Edith, Greg Spaulding (The acting PCV Director) and Betty Mwaungulu. Betty was responsible for writing reports on Peace Corps activities and sending them to Washington D.C. I guess you could call her the Peace Corps', Public Relations person.

I was still feeling weak, but knew I needed to go through with this ceremony, and become an official PCV before I could proceed to the next step, whatever was awaiting me in Biriwiri! The Acting Ambassador who swore me in was from Colorado. We had a nice visit, reminiscing about Colorado.

I came away no longer a PCT but a <u>real</u> PCV just like my peers.

Chapter Eight

Biriwiri, "My Home Away From Home"

Wellington, the training coordinator for the Peace Corps, drove me to my new site, Biriwiri. He knew I had been ill. He seemed rather in awe of me. I could not figure out why? Perhaps it was because I was older and he was not used to a white agogo. I was still not feeling 100 percent but was anxious to get started on my assignment and fend for myself.

Leaving Malanda and the protection of Madalo and Linly was a little scary for me. Madalo gave me a bag of Irish potatoes. Linly's sister, Enifa, who lived next door to Madalo and Linly, gave me five hen eggs. Gold could not have pleased me more. I carefully carried those five eggs and the bag of Irish potatoes everywhere I went, knowing how precious they were and that they would keep me from going hungry until I learned to cook Malawi style.

Leaving the main highway, Wellington steered the Peace Corps van down a rough unpaved path into a small clearing. On the right I could see the Health Center. On the left there were three small brick houses with tin roofs. The area appeared deserted. We descended from the van and I dutifully followed Wellington to meet whomever I needed to meet and hoped they would be welcoming to a new Peace Corps Volunteer.

I mentally practiced the protocol I had been instructed to follow. First impressions are so important in any culture. I did not want to start off on the wrong foot. I knew Biriwiri had had three volunteers before me, all young women. How would the people receive an older woman? What would be their expectations? Would I have the skills and ability to meet their expectations? Would they always be comparing me to the previous volunteers?

Wellington started walking toward one of the brick houses, stopped a few feet away and called out the traditional greeting, "Odi" (Hello, is anyone home?). As we waited for the woman to come to the door, I looked around. A cement porch covered with pots of flowering plants made a welcoming entrance to the house. A small garden grew next to the house and chickens scurried out of the way as we approached.

The door opened and a tall woman dressed in a white nurses uniform stepped out. Wellington introduced me to the woman and told me she was Mrs. Banali, the head nurse at the Health Centre. Mrs. Banali looked me over as if, "Now what have they brought me?" Again, I wondered what I was replacing? Did she see me as another problem or a helping hand?

It was mid-afternoon, the village appeared deserted. The children at the village were still in school. This accounted for the absence of children, but where were the adults? Mrs. Banali, apparently was on her afternoon break.. I wondered how many hidden eyes were watching me with curiosity about the new volunteer?

Mrs. Banali waved us toward the second house, which was surrounded with a grass fence and led us through the rickety grass gate. She procured a bundle of keys from her pocket and unlocked the door. I stepped over the door sill and was appalled. I remembered the clean, neat, house of Linly's and this house was filthy, like any house which has been left unattended. The last occupant, Cecelia a Peace Corps Volunteer, had left several months previously to travel around Africa before returning to the states. The wind had blown dirt and dust in through the cracks around the windows. Cobwebs and dust filled the rooms. I could not tell what color the walls were supposed to be.

The house consisted of four rooms with an inside toilet, shower and kitchen. It was one of four similar houses designated strictly for Health Care Workers. It was a brick house with a tin roof and cement floors, not the mud hut I was expecting. I knew I should be grateful, for that. However, I did not have anything to clean the house and told Wellington I could not stay in it or I would be ill again. Mrs. Banali summoned a hospital worker and ordered him to sweep and mop the floor. This helped a little.

I unlocked a bedroom and saw there was a bed with a foam mattress and a chest of drawers. The room was a treasure chest of many useful things such as a plastic bucket, a cooking pot, and dishes. One bucket with a lid was filled with spices. When I opened it a spicy aroma filled the air. I silently blessed Cecilia for leaving me such an unexpected gift. A mosquito net hung over the bed. I pulled it down amid a shower of dust and dead bugs.

All of the rooms were crowded with furniture that was not very useful. A woven mat covered the living room floor. When I lifted it there was a pattern of the rug in the dust on the floor. Geckos scurried across the top of the walls near the iron sheet ceiling. Dark streaks ran down the walls from their excrement. The doors were covered with bits of scotch tape from having pictures posted on them by the previous young PCVs. The kitchen was dark and smoky. It had a waist high fire place with a soot filled chimney to the outside. There was no running water although the house was plumbed for running water. The toilet operated by pouring water into the upper chamber then flushing it. The contents flowed into a septic tank buried in the back yard. The shower was just a room with a drain in it. We had been told the house was ready for me to move in.

The only redeeming feature in the house was a bookcase filled with 169 books with a variety of titles; Mitchner's Texas, The Celestine Prophecy, The Hobit, The Alchemist, The Bell Jar, these I had read but could now re-read. Other familiar authors were, Atwood, Hemingway, John McFee, Paul Theroux, Camus, Thoreau, Leo Tolstoy, Dostovsky, Dalai Lama, Mother Theresa, Saul Bellow, Ken Follet, Agatha Christie, Johnathon Swift, Judith Krantz, Herman Hesse, D. H. Lawrence, Kurt Vonegart, Solzhenitsyn, Shakespeare, Barbara Bradford etc. I was in readers heaven. It was like finding old friends. I love to read and now I had two years to read these books! The weevils, who had riddled the wood around the window screens had eaten only one book.

I told Wellington I would ride back with him and negotiate with Edith, my APCD (Administrator Peace Corps Department) in charge of Community Health, to see if there was another assignment that would be better for me. I had been given K9000 ($70) to help me settle in which I knew would not go far in making this particular house livable. I longed for a mud hut like Linly's sparse, primitive, but clean!

My conversation with Edith was not fruitful. I was told that three other young PCVs had been assigned to Biriwiri prior to me and she had thought an older person would be more helpful. I am a sucker for feeling needed and fell for that line of reasoning.

After all, I had told her to put me where being an older person would be an advantage. The carrot she offered me was that the house had a ground or land line phone. The only phone within miles. I did not even have a cell phone so the thought of having a phone appealed to me. I resigned myself to being assigned to Biriwiri.

Having a land line phone became an illusion over the next two years. When I went into Ntcheu to the Telephone Bureau to have the phone connected, I was told that the last PCV had left an outstanding bill of K4,000 (about $30). I contacted the Peace Corps office to see if they would pay the bill so I could have the phone connected. The P.C. office refused and I had to use part of my meager allowance to pay the bill and clear the records in order to have the phone put in my name.

After a few weeks of using the phone, I picked it up one day and there was no dial tone. Taking Gift, a new Malawian friend, with me this time I went into Ntcheu to the Telephone Bureau. I told the gentleman in charge that my phone was not working.

"I know, Madam" he replied politely.

Impatiently I said, "Well what is wrong with my phone?"

"Someone stole the poles, Madam" he replied contritely.

I looked at him in dismay and started to laugh. Then, I realized he was serious. I stifled my laugh and said, " When will the poles be replaced and my service re-established?"

"The repair truck is in the shop, Madam."

"When will the truck be fixed?"

"Next week, Madam."

I hadn't been in Malawi long, but had already learned that a person was told what they wanted to hear which was not necessarily the truth.

I sighed and left the Bureau with Gift. On the way home I said, "Does that type of thing happen often...stealing the telephone poles?"

"Oh, yes" replied Gift. "They cut them down to use for firewood. No one else has a phone so they do not see the need for the poles. And the telephone wire is very useful for clothes lines and other things."

"Why do not they use steel poles?" I queried?

Gift laughed, "They would cut them down and make hoes and shovels to sell at the market."

Still in a problem solving mode I said, " Well they need to do like we did in America in the old frontier days and hire some of the myriad of unemployed youth at the market to "ride shotgun" along the lines and prevent people from stealing the poles. That would seem more cost effective than needing to replace the poles so often and leaving people without services."

Nothing practical was ever done about the missing poles and my phone functioned sporadically. When it did not work I just shrugged my shoulders and said to myself, "Someone has stolen the poles again!"

Before my return trip to Biriwiri, after my talk with Edith, I splurged my kwacha on some paint, a bolt of white cotton cloth, a treadle sewing machine, a two burner kerosene stove, a tea kettle and lots of candles. I also stopped at the ShopRite store and loaded up on groceries and cleaning supplies. The Land Rover was bursting at its seams, but I knew that future trips would be few and far between and I had to make the most of this privilege of having free transportation.

Feeling better prepared and determined to not be a quitter, I returned to Biriwiri ready to set to work. My first task was to have my Peace Corps driver take me to the Ntcheu District Hospital to introduce myself to the District doctor, Dr.Ngoma and the Hospital Administrator, Mr. Mkandawire. This was a courtesy visit, and protocol the Peace Corps expected me to follow. The District Hospital was about ten miles past my site, Biriwiri. I walked into the hospital and was depressed at the drab environment. The walls were a dull gray. I could not tell if the walls had been painted gray or if they were gray because they were cement and had not been painted. There was an odor that was unpleasant not medicinal. Like old Lysol had been used to mop the floors. Being a psych nurse, I thought to myself, "How could anyone get well in such depressing surroundings?"

I had not contacted the people I was supposed to see so I did not know if they would be available. However, an orderly, noticed me looking lost and ushered me into the office of Mr. Mkandawire, the hospital Administrator. We were soon joined by Dr. Ngoma. Both men seemed very pleasant and friendly. We exchanged amenities and Dr. Ngoma, a large obese young man, moved to sit close to me, leaned over in a very friendly manner and explained, "That we were all like a large family." Mr. Mkandawire grinned knowingly at me and I did not know what to make of this conversation. I felt as if I was being "hit on" and I could not understand what was happening. Was I supposed to be flattered with this unwanted attention? Was this a cultural thing? Surely they realized I was an elderly woman not a young innocent volunteer like they had had before me? I jumped up and made some excuse to leave and abruptly left the meeting. Perhaps I was still not feeling well and misunderstood what was happening, but I could not stay in the room. As I found my way out of the hospital and back to the Peace Corps van I realized I had probably blown it for any thing I would need from both of those men in the future!

Later, when I contacted the District Hospital to see if I could hire their painter to completely paint the inside of my house, after many delays, a Mr. Wazeri was sent to me. Mr. Wazeri was a polite man in his fifties who spoke excellent English and told me proudly that he had eight children. I trusted him instantly. He looked over my house and told me he could paint everything in about three days. I was skeptical about this time schedule, but agreed he could start. We negotiated for K940 a day. He stayed for three months. I kept finding things for him to do. He was such a delightful man. We became good friends. I learned a lot about the history of Malawi as we worked together to bring order and cleanliness to my house. Mr. W. hired another young man to help him. I called his helper," the little painter" because I could not properly pronounce his name, Nkung'untha.

Mr. W. painted the walls of my new house a blue called "Spirit River" and the doors and trim white. It took three coats of paint to get the doors to actually look white. While Mr. W. and the little painter painted, I used the treadle machine to make cottage curtains for all the rooms.

Cottage curtains in author's living room

I pulled the dusty, weevil riddled wooden screens from the windows and Mr. Wazeri made small screens to fit the windows and keep out the mosquitoes.

I gave away most of the extra furniture in the house until I came to a piece that had MG carved into the wood. I asked Mr. Wazeri what MG meant? He said it stood for Malawi Government. I left that piece in place! Then, as a finishing touch I had the cement floor painted oxide red.

The carpenter made a wooden front gate to replace the grass gate which was disintegrating and dragging on the ground. I painted it with the blue paint. I made the gate swing shut by fastening a bungee cord on it. I wondered why bungee cords were on my list of things to bring to Malawi? I had found at least one use for them!

Now my little house was red, white, and blue. I called it my little Peace Corps House.

I asked Mr. Mkanda and Gift (the little painter) if they would make a path from my porch to my new gate. They estimated how much it would cost for the bricks and rocks and set to work promptly. I was amazed at the finished product. It was a work of art. The bricks were laid in a pattern and the rocks must have contained mica because they glistened in the sun. Now when it rained I could cross my muddy (grass free) yard and not track mud into the house. Why did not more people have brick paths into their houses?

Note the artistry that went into making the author's path!

Still finding projects for Mr. Wazeri to do, I asked Mr. Wazeri if he knew how to lay ceramic tile? I wanted the top of the cement kitchen counter and up the wall a foot or so tiled so I could keep the kitchen cleaner. Mr. W. came every day to work on my house on the minibus from Ntcheu, which was ten miles each way. I knew this was costing him money so I asked him if he would like to have a bicycle (njinga) and if he was fit enough to ride it from Ntcheu. I was not certain if he could manage the hills surrounding Biriwiri. He was positive he could manage so we made a verbal contract. He would tile my kitchen for a bicycle (jinga). I was delighted with our contract. The first day, after purchasing his bicycle, he rode 80 kilometers, the equivalent of about 40 miles. I was amazed.

All I needed now was the tile. How I got the tile is another story of itself. I knew I could not manage to buy tile and bring it back to Biriwiri by myself. Still new to the customs, I asked Dorothy, the leader of the women's group, if she would go with me to Blantyre to find tile. Since she was in need of some sewing supplies for her women she was happy to accompany me. She asked if Rose, another woman in the sewing group could go with us. I knew this meant paying minibus fees for the three of us and also buying lunch, still I welcomed their assistance and it would be worth it in the long run. I was thinking of how heavy the tile would be, plus the grout. An extra pair of strong arms would be welcome.

It was eight o'clock in the morning when we caught a minibus for Blantyre the following day. Arriving in Blantyre after a three hour ride on a crowded minibus, we went first to a sewing shop and made our purchases. By this time it was noon and we were famished. We found a little café and the women ordered chips and a coke. I ordered the same, the chips were greasy but filling. After lunch we looked for a tile store and were told in a hardware shop the tile store was across town. The man in the shop offered to take us to the store in his truck. Since Rose and Dorothy were with me I reasoned I could accept his offer and it would be safe.

The tile shop was very busy. I picked out a blue tile, paid for it, and asked the manager to call a taxi for us to transport the tile and ourselves back to the bus station. The manager did not seem to understand what I was wanting and I repeated my request. I realized later what an empirical thing my request had been. I had just proved myself to be the "Ugly American" I so despised. The store had a phone. I could see it on the wall, but there was no way for it to connect to a cab! I was not in America! I had a lot to learn about how to conduct myself in Malawi!

Dorothy, hearing me talking to the manager, came to my rescue and said she would find a taxi and strode off to find one. I was told to wait with Rose and the boxes of tile. Soon Dorothy returned in the taxi and we were taken to the bus stop. By now it was evening. We climbed on the last bus and found seats. At last we could relax and were on our way home, another three hour ride.

About half-way home the bus stopped at a cross roads and the conductor asked everyone to get off because he was turning at the cross roads. I had paid the full fare and expected to be transported back to Biriwiri. But instead, we were dumped unceremoniously beside the road. It was beginning to get dark. Always the problem solver and undaunted, Dorothy decided we should cross the road and wait for another bus to come along. Rose was not saying anything because she did not understand English. I was following Dorothy's lead in everything, after being very humbled by my "taxi" gaffe. Carrying our heavy boxes of ceramic tile we crossed the road and stood waiting expectantly for another bus.

This trip was now becoming an adventure as we stood waiting for a bus or minibus, not knowing when or if one would come. The moon came up and it was almost light as day.

A huge lorry stopped on our side of the road. I could see men on the open back which was piled high with sacks of grain. Some of the men got off to relieve themselves by the side of the road. They were quietly laughing and joking with each other. Dorothy grabbed my hand and said, "Come on." Before I could grasp what she was doing, she scrambled up the wheel, which was taller than my head, and asked me to hand her one of the boxes of tile. I complied then wondered how I could mount those tires? Apparently this was being expected of me. Also, was what she was doing illegal? While I was still pondering this daring act, Rose handed up her box of tile and scrambled up on the bed of the truck then turned and offered a hand to pull me up. Once on the truck, the men ignored us and we settled down on the bags of grain. The night air was warm and we were comfortable. Dorothy leaned into the back window of the truck and asked the driver what the fare would be and told him where to let us off.

As we rumbled off, finally on our way home, I laughed to myself and wondered, "Who in my family or friends would ever believe that this elderly woman, me, was riding on the back of a Lorry, in the middle of the night, in Africa, with perfect strangers?" At the same time I felt perfectly safe and was thoroughly enjoying myself. I wondered who was caring for Rose and Dorothy's children. I did not think we would be gone so long. Dorothy and Rose did not seem to be concerned. I guess extended family steps in when needed in emergencies like this.

It was 2 a.m. when with a squeal of the powerful air brakes, the Lorry stopped at Biriwiri. The men helped us down off the Lorry and handed down the boxes of tile. Dorothy and Rose balanced a box of tile each on their heads then handed me the box of grout and started down the sloping rough path to my house. I put the box of grout on my head and followed their footsteps down the rough path.

Happy to be back in Biriwiri, I felt giddy from my adventure, and skipped down the path like a school girl to my front door, where faithful Mary had a candle burning in the window to welcome me home. Home at last.

The tail lights of the Lorry disappeared in the distance.

A compilation of pictures for the reader to enjoy.

The author's kitchen before it was painted and tiled

The "little painter" and Mr. Wazeri tiling the kitchen

Kitchen after being remodeled. Note the tin exhaust hood over the kerosene stove and cabinets with doors instead of open shelves

Completed Guardian Shelter. Note the precision of the brick work done only with a string and a level. A small porch with two plastic chairs are on the front

Inside the completed Guardian Shelter. One room of three beds is for female guardians, one room of three beds is for men. The kitchen has a sink, running water and an electric hot plate

Traditional healer with her herbs

Enifa, the author, Linly and Tendai in front of
Linly's house

Alick Kadosa and the author

Ox cart which carried a woman in labor to the clinic

Fred, our safari guide, and his truck

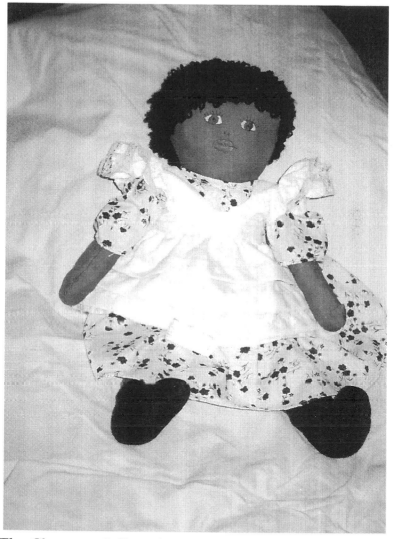

The Chamaso doll made by the Biriwiri Women's Group
(Later dolls did not have the apron)

Chapter Nine

Mary, My Brown Angel

Shortly after moving into my little house, Mrs. Banali and some of the nurses from the Health Centre visited me, bringing a young girl with them.

Mrs. Banali introduced her, saying, "This is Mary. She can work for you."

A neatly dressed, sturdy girl, Mary's clear, dark skin had a healthy glow, like "honey with the sun shining through it," as I have heard healthy, dark skin described. Not dull or ashen, like some Malawians who were malnourished or ill. Mary was 20 years old. She had worked for two of the previous PCVs. I made a mental note that she must have been around 15 when she started working away from home. This meant she was probably reliable and experienced.

In orientation we had talked about having a worker, usually a night watchman. Part of our allowance from the Peace Corps was designated for hiring a watchman. This person slept on the veranda of a PCV's house and kept the PCV safe from thieves, mischievous children, and marauding animals. Having a watchman was one way for someone to have a job, and working for a PCV carried with it some status. I knew that if I hired Mary it would give her an income, which she would share with her family. Job opportunities were scarce, especially for a girl, in Biriwiri. With Mary around, I probably would not need a watchman! She looked strong enough to frighten away any potential intruder, man or beast.

I said, "And what can you do for me, Mary?"

Mary replied, "I can clean your house, carry water, wash your clothes, go to the market, and cook your meals."

I said, "I will probably cook my own meals. I need to learn how to do that. How much would you want me to pay you?"

We agreed on K900 ($7.00) a month and a trial of one month. After that we would negotiate extending her contract or terminating it. By the time I left Biriwiri I had increased Mary's salary to K1200 ($9.50) She was worth every kwacha!

I wondered whether stories of my peculiar American ways would be circulated in the village. For instance, sniffing at food was considered very rude. I always smelled an egg when I cracked it to see if it was fresh. The first time I did this, Mary laughed and told me it was simply not done. I think it must have seemed to Malawians like a dog or animal sniffing. I appreciated being told about things that were cultural taboos. I did not know, then, how loyal Mary would be. I do not think she ever shared stories of what went on in my house, but instead paved the way for my integration into the Biriwiri community.

Mary sitting on authors' porch, reading

Hiring Mary was the smartest thing I did during my assignment. Not only was Mary a good worker, honest, reliable, and pleasant, but her biggest asset was that she knew everyone in the village. She was a fountain of knowledge and common sense wisdom. When I needed something done, I would ask Mary who in the village had the skill or knowledge, and she would take care of it.

An example of her folk wisdom is when my little brown hen, which was given to me by the woman traditional healer, was missing. I thought a hyena had probably eaten her. But Mary said, "Do not worry. She will probably come back with some baby chicks."

Sure enough in a few weeks she appeared with five chicks. I was so happy.

The first time I needed to go into Lilongwe on a minibus by myself I was very apprehensive. During our initial training, an older PCV had threatened us with "being sent home" if we did not practice riding on a minibus during our training period. Somehow, I had missed the opportunity to practice. Now I was going by myself on this scary trip. Mary must have sensed my nervousness. She walked with me to the M1 and stood with me, waiting for a bus. Our trainers had told us what to look for in choosing a bus that was safe to ride. Those instructions are ignored when you just need to get some place and do not have many options to choose from.

As we stood waiting with many other people also waiting for a bus, I noticed a nicely dressed Malawian young woman standing a little apart from the rest of us. I thought, *She must be waiting for a particular ride. That is why she is standing so far away.* About that time, a small white van covered with Johnson and Johnson product logos pulled up by her and the woman climbed into the van. The driver must be a salesman/distributor for Johnson and Johnson, I mused.

Before I knew what was happening, Mary grabbed my arm and dragged me to the van, opened the door and pushed me in almost on top of the woman already in the van. Mary's actions seemed very rude and I apologized to the driver for my pushy entrance into his van. However, the driver did not seem too surprised. The woman said, "I will sit in the back," and climbed over the seat to the back seat.

Trying to remember the protocol we had been taught, I asked, "How much will this ride be?" The driver said, "K200, I guess, but I do have to make one stop in Dedza."

As he pulled into the traffic and accelerated, I turned to get a good look at my chauffeur. I said, "Did anyone ever tell you that you look like Will Smith? Do you know who Will is?" The young man ducked his head, smiled, and with a pork pie hat perched jauntily on his head, making him look even more like Will, he replied, "Yes, I have heard that, and yes I have seen his movies." He introduced himself as Mike. I told him I was with the Peace Corps.

For the next two hours, we chatted about Will and the experiences Mike had had in his life. Mike had a degree in business and was very happy with his job as a Johnson and Johnson sales representative. The woman in the back remained quiet even when we stopped in Dedza for almost an hour.

Mike drove me to the gate to the Peace Corps office and let me out. I walked into the office and bragged, "Guess who I hitched a ride with?" For a few minutes everyone believed I had actually ridden with Will Smith!

I never saw Mike again.

Another time when I had to go into Lilongwe, I took Mary with me. It was dark by the time we got home on the minibus. When we got off the bus at Biriwiri I realized I had forgotten my flashlight. Clinging to each other in the pitch blackness, we started down the rough incline leading to my house. I heard a drunk staggering home on the other side of the road. Mary froze. I am sure she thought it was a ghost or some evil spirit who would probably snatch one or both of us. Then I heard her say, "There is someone behind us with a torch." It was a great relief to hear the familiar voice of Mr. Ligogo say, "I heard the bus stop and figured it must be the two of you." He guided us safely to our door. I vowed never to forget my flashlight again!

I had my flashlight with me a second time when Mary and I again came home after dark. Mary said, "Put the light over there." She pointed in a direction for the light to follow. The light picked up a small hedgehog waddling along in his nightly search for grubs and insects. I had never seen a real hedgehog before; only pictures in Beatrix Potter's story books. I was thrilled to see the tiny night creature.

I was glad she was not pointing out a snake for me to regard. The snakes become active at night. I certainly did not want to encounter a snake. I never did see a snake at any time during my stay in Malawi. I considered myself lucky. My friend Kathy had a spitting cobra in her yard, which her counterpart promptly killed. Mike and Amy, our newlyweds, were greeted with a Mamba on their doorstep the day they arrived at their new site. The villagers killed the snake and took it away, assuring Mike and Amy that it was the *only* snake around! A Mamba is one of the most deadly snakes in Africa. Enough about snakes.

Mary did not stay overnight at my house unless I was going to be gone overnight. On such occasions, I paid her K100 each night to act as my night watchman. I had the carpenter make a twin size wooden bed for Mary for when she needed to stay over.

The carpenter was illiterate. He seemed very uncomfortable around me. He measured the mattress I had purchased on my last trip into Lilongwe to see how long to make the bed without unrolling the rolled up mattress completely. I silently questioned his accuracy of measurement but did not say anything. I knew he would not understand my English, and would be even more uncomfortable. Mary was not around to help interpret for me.

When the carpenter delivered the bed, a few days later, it was too short by about two inches. A four-inch-thick foam mattress made the bed very comfortable, and the two inches that hung over the foot of the bed were not noticeable. The bed was painted with varnish to discourage the weevils from eating it.

A friend in the states sent me a set of blue sheets and a mattress cover. I made a quilt as a top cover for the bed from scraps my friends sent to me for sewing projects. I purchased a pillow and made a pillowcase for it. Now when Mary had to stay overnight when I was gone, she had a comfortable place to sleep.

Most Malawians sleep on the floor on a pallet or reed mat, which they roll up in the morning and store against the wall. Having a bed and mattress is a luxury. Mary returned to her village when my tour was up. She took the bed and its linens with her.

Mary and I became good friends. We made decisions together. I did not feel she was a servant, and did not ask her to do anything I was not willing to do myself. Mary was very proud of her ability to carry water on her head. She could carry a wash tub of water on her head without spilling a drop. Her neck muscles were strong. Her posture was erect and regal. Her arms were like small logs of wood, taut and hard. She loved children, and they loved her. One child in particular would follow her, carrying a small container of water on his own head.

Malawians do not like grass. Mary liked the grass to be short and sparse in my yard so she could sweep the yard with a small bundle of branches. This act reminded me of the "house proud" women, when I was living in Scotland, whose last task before setting out to market each day was to white-wash the front steps. A white-washed stoop was a sign of a good wife and housekeeper in Scotland. A swept, clean yard in Biriwiri was a sign of a "house proud" homemaker.

Once, when I was called away on Peace Corps business, I returned to find a very distraught Mary. Someone had stolen eight of my fat hybrid chickens. I had chased two teenage boys out of my yard a few days prior to this incident. I wondered what they were wanting. It did not occur to me that they had been scouting out my chicken house!

Mary was so upset that the chickens had been stolen on her watch. The chicken house was outside her bedroom window, but she did not hear the stealthy thieves. The thieves propped the blue gate open with a stone. It was a clear, moonlit night almost as bright as day. The thieves carefully removed some of the bricks from the chicken house and reached in to retrieve the sleeping chickens. Sleeping chickens do not make a noise when lifted off their roost and placed in a mealie bag (like a gunny sack).

The next day Mary went to the market twice to see if she could find the chickens. She thought the thieves would likely sell the chickens and she would recognize our chickens. No luck, so it was a tearful Mary that met me with the bad news. I learned later that several people had had some chickens stolen on that moonlit night.

A year or so after I returned to the states, I heard through one of my Malawi friends that the chicken thieves had been caught and given eight years in jail for their thieving ways. This seemed a little harsh to me, but I had never encountered the justice system in Malawi. Now a precious cow would seem to warrant such a sentence, but chickens?

Author's little chicken house. (Later the ladder and door were painted blue)

When the Youth Club wanted to start a pre-school, I asked Mary if she would like to be one of the teachers. She was delighted. We had almost 40 children, ages 2-5, enrolled. I wanted one teacher for every ten students. Two other young women, Letia and Sherifa were recruited. A young male, Blessing, was also hired. His parents were so happy we had asked him to help. He was only 18, and there was nothing else for him to do in the village except get into trouble. Being a teacher would keep him occupied. His little brother was one of the 40 students.

My friend, Mary Ann, who had started a pre-school in her village, asked whether she could provide a teaching workshop for the teachers I had recruited. My counterpart and several others in the village, including the four teachers, were interested in learning how to run a pre-school. Mary Ann's school was very successful. The headmaster at the primary school in her village had complimented Mary Ann on how well prepared the children from her school were when they entered primary school.

I was not able to accompany the people who attended Mary Ann's workshop. They returned very excited over the things they had learned. Mary Ann had fed them lunch and gave each of them a certificate of attendance. My Mary was so proud of her certificate. She bustled with enthusiasm as she told me how the day went. Working as a certified teacher gave her an additional K400 a month. She went to the school in the morning, and came to my house in the afternoon to do chores for me.

Tuesday was market day. The market was a mile away, next to the MI. Mary and I would sit down the night before and decide what I needed. Mary would estimate how much my list would cost. Then, kwacha in hand, (or rather tied in a corner of her chitenje) off to market she would go, carrying a basket for her purchases.

Mary loved to go to the market. She visited with her friends, and haggled with the vendors much better than I could. For her, going to the market was like going to a county fair. The market became a hub of activity with people, oxen carts, goats, chickens, pigs, cattle, and other animals from all over the Ntcheu district.

People brought their wares to the market to sell. Some vendors had stalls for their things, while other spread a reed mat on the ground and sold their products, like vegetables or hand-made crafts. The vendors would take one look at me and the price of their wares would double! Having Mary do the marketing was cost-effective for me!

I needed to be careful how much I was asking Mary to carry home. Kerosene for the stove was very heavy. If it was not available at the market, Mary would go to Ntcheu to purchase it. Ntcheu was ten miles away. She did not like to disappoint me.

The first time I sent Mary to the market, she left early in the morning and by 5 PM was still not home. Soon it would be dark. I went next door to Mrs. Banali and told her I thought something had happened to Mary. I had visions of her being beaten by some of the hoodlums at the market, hit by a minibus, robbed and afraid to come home and tell me, or some equally tragic disaster had befallen her. Mrs. Banali sent one of her children to look for Mary but assured me she thought Mary was probably safe. Shortly afterwards Mary came sauntering into the yard. I was so relieved to see her I could not scold her. She reminded me of the young colored girl, in the movie *Gone With the Wind,* who was sent to fetch the doctor and took her time returning, causing Scarlett to panic.

When I complained about the geckos running up the walls and leaving tell-tale marks on my beautiful new blue paint, Mary told me a story of why geckos are welcomed in Malawian houses. They keep down the insect population, but also listen and know what goes on in a house. In the story, this latter ability won the hand of the King's daughter. It was a gecko on the wall of the castle who was listening and heard the King and his wife talking, that could answer the proverbial question which puzzled the other suitors. I quit complaining until one night when I went to bed, I found a tiny, baby gecko on my pillow. I carried the pillow to the front door and deposited him unceremoniously outside!

One day I found evidence of a mouse in my kitchen. Mary went to the market and returned with a tiny packet of rat poison. She sprinkled it on a cut tomato and placed it on the floor. The next morning there was a huge mouse, or possibly a small rat, lying by the tomato. I never had any more rodents in my house.

My house had bats in it. I could never figure out where they stayed during the day, but when it got dark they would come out. If they could not find a way to the outside, they would fly around and bump into things. The saying, "Blind as a bat" seemed very appropriate. I would open the door and use my broom to try to shoo them outside. They were very small, probably no bigger than four inches from wingtip to wingtip. I did not want to kill them, because they were very useful to keep down the mosquito population.

Sitting reading by my little kerosene lamp one evening, I had a weird sensation that made me say to myself, *I am not alone in this house!* My senses had picked up the movement of air in a corner of the room. Sure enough, a tiny bat was in the room.

Occasionally, when I tired of chasing them, I just went to bed and pulled the covers over my head until morning. In the light of day they were gone, back to where they stayed, probably under the eaves of my house or in the chimney.

Although Mary had a lot of common sense and natural wisdom, she was very into spirits and bewitching. There were some small birds that ran across my tin roof and made an audible racket. Mary said they were spirits. I thought she was kidding at first. When she continued to label them as spirits, I grabbed her by the arm and took her outside and pointed to the birds on the roof. I am not sure I convinced her, but she did not mention spirits on my roof again.

It was very unusual for a Malawian girl to not have a baby, married or not, especially by the time a girl was Mary's age. Mary's friend, Letia, one of the teachers in the pre-school, had a two-year-old son, Clement. Letia never told me, but I believe she was impregnated by one of her teachers. It was common for a teacher to use his position of authority to convince a young girl to have sex with him.

Mary and Letia were sitting in my house giggling and reading a health publication which listed some of the myths about sex commonly believed to be true in their culture. One of the myths was that sex was the only way a girl could get Vitamin K, which was essential for good health. The publication disputed this myth and said it was untrue.

Letia asked, "Is this truly a myth or is it true?"

I said, "Vitamin K comes from eating leafy green vegetables. It is a myth perpetuated to fool young girls into having sex."

Mary said skeptically, "But girls who have sex always look so happy and have such rosy cheeks!"

I said firmly, "That has nothing at all to do with Vitamin K!"

Another myth commonly believed, especially by men, is that having sex with a virgin will cure a man of HIV. It is myths like these that spread the virus of AIDs, and make it so difficult to teach "Behavioral change."

When my time with the Peace Corps was finished, no other Peace Corps Volunteers were assigned to Biriwiri. Mary returned to her parents' home in another village, where she used what she had learned at Biriwiri and started her own pre-school. I keep in touch with her. She has hired two of her sisters to help her, and seems to be doing very well. She is still not married, and does not have any children of her own.

I learned so much from Mary. She made my life in Biriwiri so much easier. I do not know how I would have survived without her.

She truly was my brown angel.

Chapter Ten

Meeting my Counterpart and Getting to Work

Peace Corps protocol gave us three months to get settled in our assigned village. In that time, we were supposed to complete a community assessment to find out what the health needs of the community were, and, in conjunction with the community, make plans to address these needs.

I had been at Biriwiri a few weeks and was happily in the middle of fixing up my house, when the head honcho, Mr. Kwanjana, summoned me to his office in the Health Centre. I think Mr. Kwanjana thought I was stalling about getting started in the "real" work of the Peace Corps. And, perhaps I was stalling. I was not sure what I was supposed to be doing. I felt that my being sick had made me miss some very important information that would have guided me in getting started. I had no one to talk to about this. My peers were at other sites, and seemed busy doing something. People have asked me what it felt like being the only white person for miles. I never gave it a thought. So far, it had not hampered whatever I needed to do. I always had Mary and Dorothy, the leader of the women's group, to smooth the way for me. I loved both of them, and they both accepted me unconditionally. The reader will meet Dorothy in the next chapter.

Mr. Kwanjana had stopped by to see me when I arrived at Biriwiri to welcome me. I had not had a conversation with him since that first day. He was a tall man with a rugged, kind face. He reminded me of the actor Danny Glover. I liked him immediately. He had been stationed at Biriwiri for seven years, but wanted to be transferred closer to the city of Lilongwe. He had the respect of his peers at the Health Centre. At first I thought he was a doctor, but learned he was a very experienced nurse. Doctors are very scarce in Malawi; less than 100 in all of Malawi. Nurses run most of the Health Centres.

Feeling a little apprehensive about our first meeting, I changed from my jeans to a skirt, grabbed a notebook and pen and hurried across the common area to Mr. Kwanjana's office.

When I entered the room and bowed to Mr. Kwanjana, I noticed a slim, neatly dressed young man sitting in front of the desk. Mr. Kwanjana introduced me to the man as my assigned counterpart, Mr. Ligogo. A counterpart is responsible for the person assigned to him. In my case he kept me out of trouble many times by slowing me down when I rushed into projects with out giving due consideration to the proper cultural protocol. I learned that Mr. Ligogo had worked with at least two of the previous volunteers at Biriwiri. His wife was the postmistress at Biriwiri. He had two small children. Speaking excellent English, he said he would help me with the language by acting as a translator. Only the health care workers and a few others in the village spoke English.

Lyson Ligogo on the author's front porch

Mr. K. started our talk by telling me about the services that were offered at the Health Clinic, the schedule of the clinics, etc. He shared with me what the other Peace Corps Volunteers who had been assigned to Biriwiri had done for the community. He said, "Now what you can do for us is to use whatever influence you have to get people to accept the "scientific method" of health care, instead of going to the traditional healers." I was dismayed with the enormity of this assignment but kept quiet.

He told me a story of a woman who came to the clinic with an eye infection; pink eye. Pink eye (conjunctivitis) can be easily treated with antibiotics, but if left untreated usually runs its course in about ten days. It is very contagious, and if a person does not use good hand-washing, it can be easily spread to another person. It is also unsightly and uncomfortable. Mr. K. gave the woman an eye antibiotic ointment and told her how to use it and to return in two weeks. The woman went back to her village and was met by a traditional healer who looked at the medicine she had been given and said. "This won't heal your eyes. What you need is penicillin." Penicillin is considered the "magic bullet" by the uninformed, a cure for almost any illness.

Upon hearing that she needed penicillin, the woman went to Mozambique, across the MI from Malawi, and purchased a bottle of injectable penicillin. She pried off the top and filled the bottle with un-sterile water. She then used the solution as eye drops for two weeks. When she returned to the clinic her vision was badly impaired. The cornea was burned and scarred from using the potent and unsterile Penicillin. Mr. K. had tears in his eyes as he said, "There was nothing I could do for her. She is almost blind from such a simple illness.

I would like to never see something like that happen again."

I was stunned. He was asking me to change a entire culture's belief about health care. Most of the people were Christian, but their basic beliefs were more animistic (a belief in spirits and magic). I was not so sure I put all my faith in "the scientific method" myself. I believe the mind and body worked together. Some seemingly "unscientific" methods work just fine. Besides, I had not conducted my community assessment, as ordered by the Peace Corps. What would I tell my APCD, Edith, in my quarterly report? I was going by the book! I thought, *If three other PCV's have each done a community assessment, then this community has been thoroughly assessed, and Mr. K., who has been here seven years, surely knows what this community needs. I am here to do what the community needs for me to do.*

I took a deep breath and said, "I am not sure what I can do, but let me think about it and I will get back to you. I need to consult with my new counterpart."

I talked with Mr. Ligogo, and together we decided we needed to find out more about the traditional healers who practiced in the Biriwiri catchment area, which consisted of twenty-two small villages. I discovered there were seventeen traditional healers in all. Three were in the village of Biriwiri. We devised a survey of questions we needed to ask each healer. Our main concern was the use of "sharps" to treat various illnesses. Small cuts to the forehead with a sharp razor blade are a treatment that traditional healers use for severe headaches. We wondered if a clean sharp was used between patients. If not, this is one way HIV could be transmitted.

Together, we visited the three healers in our village. Then I was called back to Lilongwe for a PCV seminar. When I returned to Biriwiri, Mr. Ligogo had finished visiting the rest of the healers. I was disappointed, because I wanted to meet all the healers. I do not know what happened to the survey. Mr. K. was transferred shortly after the survey was completed. I do not think there was any follow-up, but just talking to the healers allowed them to know we were willing to work with them and would treat them with respect. We offered to dispense clean sharps if they needed them.

Just getting the people in distant villages to accept HIV as an illness, and institute "behavioral changes" that would curb the spread of the virus was a challenge. In the distant villages, the people did not have any form of communication with the rest of Malawi. There were no telephones, radios, newspapers etc. I had the only phone. A few people had cell phones. The Health Center communicated with a short wave radio. I remembered reading in an old National Geographic magazine about what was called "the withering disease" in which African people became very thin and died. I think the illness was attributed to eating monkey meat. I wonder now whether that was the beginning of HIV in Africa.

Being sexually free was about the only entertainment the natives had. They could not in their wildest imagination connect it to HIV. Suspicious of more educated people's messages about how to conduct their lives, they resisted behavioral change and continued to believe the myths they had inherited. If a person became ill, they believed he obviously had been bewitched by someone who had contact with him. Myths are difficult to dispel, according to the mythologist Joseph Campbell. I firmly believe this.

In our training, we were taught about practices in some of the rural villages that potentiated the spread of HIV. If a man died, his wife was given to another male in the family, and the male, usually a brother, was obligated to climb into her bed in the night and have sex with her. This was supposed to help the deceased husband in some way, cleanse him in the afterlife, or something. One of our instructors told us about his experience with this tradition. His eldest brother died and he was the designated person who was told by the family he must fulfill this duty. He refused saying, "She was so much older than me that it would have been like having sex with my mother."

Another traditional practice still in vogue is the naming of a "hyena" in a village. A hyena is a man who is selected, probably by the village chief, to enter, under the cover of darkness, the bed of a young girl of marrying age and have sex with her. This act is supposed to prepare the young woman for marriage. This is another means of spreading HIV, if the hyena is infected.

I had a personal experience with the belief of bewitching. The new nurse who took Mr. Kwanjana's place believed in bewitching. I was gone from my site for several days. Upon returning I felt a change in the usually friendly people. I asked my neighbor what had happened while I was away. Her answer was that I did not need to know, and to forget about it.

Feeling that it definitely had something to do with me, I persisted and finally learned that a friend, Alice, who had been seen visiting me, was accused of bewitching the new head nurse because he became ill with Malaria. Because Alice had been seen frequently visiting my house, I was supposedly in league with Alice. I was afraid this rumor would affect my work at Biriwiri. However, the problem was solved in the usual passive aggressive way of Malawians by sending Alice to a new site. At her new site, Alice became friends with a nurse who later died. Again, poor Alice was immediately transferred to a third site. Things at Biriwiri returned to normal and I continued my work.

One of the healers we had visited in our village was a woman. Her hut was immaculate. She had several women working with her as apprentices. They sang and danced for us. Mr. Ligogo and I sat on a reed mat and showed our appreciation for their sharing with us by clapping when they were finished. I was very impressed with the "spiritual healing" method she used. I noticed several large wooden crosses in her hut and white robes that she apparently wore while treating a patient. The walls on her hut were covered with posters advocating health measures, such as boiling water before drinking it and using mosquito nets.

Several days after visiting the healer I was paid a visit by one of her apprentices. She was accompanied by Mr. Ligogo, who introduced her and explained that the woman had a gift for me from the healer. The woman carried a basket with a cloth on it. She knelt on my doorstep and removed the cloth. Huddled inside the basket was a small brown hen. This was a token of appreciation, and a gift for me. It is a custom to give a chicken to someone in Malawi. I was so pleased. I knew I was being accepted and felt honored. I put the hen in my kitchen until I could build a pen for her. That little hen gave me many fresh eggs and raised at least two broods of chicks during my stay in Biriwiri. At one time I had thirteen chickens. I felt wealthy indeed, and teased Mr. Ligogo that wealth should be measured in chickens, not in cows, like the Malawians. Cows were the Malawians bank account.

I thought about what else I could do to influence the people to come to the hospital instead of going to the traditional healers. I had been told some horror stories during my orientation about health care practices in Malawi. One story was about how a laboring woman would be slapped if she made a noise. This was particularly appalling to me as a nurse. It violated everything I ever thought a nurse should do or be. We were told there was a superior attitude among anyone who had more education than another. I saw subtle signs of this when I worked in the clinics. Women were made to attend the clinic at 7:30 A.M. But, the health care workers did not arrive until 9 A.M. No thought was given to the fact that the women had to rise early to do their chores at home; carrying water, making breakfast for a lazy husband and other children, bathe herself and her baby, and then walk several miles to the clinic to sit and wait for the clinic to open.

While waiting for the clinic to open, one HSA (Health Surveillance Attendant) would lead the women in a song that had to do with health habits, like how to recognize Malaria and how to treat it. Since most of the 100-plus women at the clinic were illiterate, health was taught through song. I tried to imagine a large pediatric clinic in America filled with mothers and children singing while they waited to see the doctor.

I'd also heard that patients were given aspirin for everything and sent home. No one seemed to trust the health care workers to treat them kindly or with respect, so they went to the traditional healers who were more accepting of them.

I thought about these things, and decided I first needed to gain the trust of the patients. I remembered the tray of hot tea I was given while in the British hospital. I felt noticed, valued, and cared for each time the aide brought me that tray. I knew I could have used a thousand words to try to convince the nurses and health workers to be more respectful and thoughtful of their patients, and woo them to the clinics, but why should they listen to this mzunga (white woman)? The only thing I had in my favor was that I was an agogo (old woman). The Malawians respect age. I decided I would show by my actions how to properly nurture someone who was sick and needing attention. I would take a cup of hot tea to the new mothers in the maternity ward! Malawian women were expected to bear children with no special consideration because of their pregnancy. They were, in fact, literally ignored and had to continue their usual work until labor started. Then they had to deliver without medication, or even a kind word.

Each mother was accompanied by a guardian, usually her mother or grandmother, who cared for the new mother and the baby during her stay in the maternity ward. Other women come to visit and sit on the floor around the laboring woman's bed. The women seemed to love to visit the health center to see a new mother and her baby. After all, there was not much else going on in the villages.

I thought, *If I take a tray of hot tea to a new mother, she will not only enjoy it, but it will stimulate the production of her milk and help to reduce her after-birth pains. My actions will be observed by the other women and soon the word will get around that the new mothers are treated nicely, with respect. Women will not want to have their babies at home to avoid coming to the Health Centre.*

I took my plan to Mr. K. and he laughed, but gave me permission to start my project. I did not want to start something that I could not continue. I reasoned I could squeeze a few kwacha for tea and sugar out of the meager allowance the Peace Corps gave us.

My worker, Mary, was interested in my project. I drew a picture of a tray for her to take to the carpenter's shop to have a suitable tray made. I put my best cups on the tray and filled a small tea pot with hot tea. I trained the nurses to hang a flag on a line outside the maternity unit to let me know how many mothers were on the unit. I made tea accordingly, and put the correct number of cups on the tray.

I arose at 5:30 each morning, when it got light. For the next two years, I faithfully carried my tea tray to the new mothers. I clucked over their new babies, and did some on-the-spot teaching with the new mothers, about caring for herself and her new baby. I am not sure how much they understood. Most of them spoke little English and my Chechewa never did get perfected. If I had a biscuit (cookie) or bun handy I added it to the tray.

Sometimes, if there were not too many mothers on the unit, I made tea for the guardians as well. At 4 PM, no matter what I was doing; in a meeting, sewing with the women, or teaching, I excused myself and went home to set up the tea tray and carried it over to the maternity unit for afternoon tea. If I was gone from my site, Mary fixed the tea. I think this was Mary's favorite task.

Mary with the tea tray for the new mothers

She knew some of the mothers, and could chat with them and admire their babies.

117

As time went on, we added embroidered cloths and nicer cups, a fancy sugar bowl, creamer, and little silver spoons. I wanted to treat the new mothers like royalty. They enjoyed the attention and soon I began getting feedback like, "Have you heard about the white woman at Biriwiri? She gave my wife hot tea when my wife had our baby." Women who were supposed to be discharged waited until they had had their morning cup of tea before going home! I hope the tea sustained them in their walk back to their village.

I wish better data had been kept on the number of admissions to the maternity ward prior to starting my tea project. I could then have had something to compare the later admissions to. A chart hung on the wall in the maternity unit, but the record was several years old. However, there were many other variables that affected the outcome of my project, such as changes in personnel and the temporary closing of the Health Centre.

I continued my tea project, much to the amusement of my Peace Corps peers, for the next two years. My P.C. peers were busy doing serious things like digging bore holes (wells) and teaching about HIV/AIDs. When I left Biriwiri, I gave the nurses an electric tea kettle with an automatic shutoff when the water boiled, and the tray with all the accouterments. I hoped they would be able to keep up the tea project. The patients would probably have to furnish their own tea, but at least they would have a hot drink on the cold days. Biriwiri did not yet have electricity, but it was rumored that it would come within the near future. I had been hearing this rumor since the first day I arrived at Biriwiri. I no longer believed the rumor.

A second project I started was to have my friends and family send me packets of baby clothes, complete with diaper pins. Many of the newborns went home wrapped in a piece of old cloth or a towel. I think the diaper pins were more valued by the mothers than the clothes. The babies were swaddled and carried on their mother's back with just their little nose peeking out at the world. I would make packets of one blanket, two diapers, two pins, a onesy, hat (if I had one), socks or bootees, and place them on the tea tray before I carried it over to the maternity unit. These things were really appreciated on a cold winter day in June or July.

I wonder how having electricity has affected the routine on the Maternity. Electricity did not arrive at Biriwiri until after I left. Instruments were previously sterilized in a pressure cooker over a charcoal stove. Women were told to bring a bar of Lifebuoy soap for their shower after delivery, which was usually in cold water. A piece of torn woolen blanket served as a vaginal pad.

Foundation for the new Guardian Shelter

A new guardian shelter has been completed. I wonder whether the guardians are using it. It has an electric hot plate that will allow the guardians to cook or re-heat a hot meal for the new mothers. The old Maternity Unit did not have a kitchen. During the rainy season it was impossible to build a fire outside to cook a hot meal. I hope the serving of hot tea has continued.

There is nothing like a cup of hot tea to lift spirits and take off the chill of cold Malawian mornings.

Chapter Eleven

The Biriwiri Women's Group

Mary and I were busy in my little house trying to get it organized and turn it into a comfortable home for me. I had decided I could do the work I was sent to do for the next two years and still be comfortable as possible. Being comfortable included having clean, neat, stimulating, and colorful surroundings. My house could be a model for anyone else of what could be done with the Spartan existence I had inherited. I was so happy to have a brick house with a tin roof and cement floor, as opposed to a mud hut with a thatched roof and dirt floor, like some of my peers. I did not feel deprived by not having electricity and running water.

As I worked in the living room, I looked out the window and saw five women coming into my yard. They pushed the gate open and walked purposefully to my front door.

I called to Mary who was working in the back bedroom, saying, "I think I am going to need your help." I thought I would need a translator.

Mary came into the living room, glanced out the window, smiled, and said, "I do not think you will need my help."

Puzzled by her comment, I opened my door and invited the women in. Dressed in colorful chitenjes with white blouses, the women radiated energy and purpose. The apparent spokesperson for the group spoke perfect English as she introduced herself to me saying, "I am Dorothy, and these women are members of our women's group here in Biriwiri."

The women took seats in my small living room smiling at me expectantly. I realized what Mary meant when she said I would not need her help! The woman who stood before me was very articulate and self-assured. Her manner toward me was as plain as if she had spoken the words out loud. *We want to meet the new volunteer sent by the Peace Corps. She is here to help everyone in this village. We want to get to her before she becomes too busy with other projects. We women need her assistance as much as anyone, so here we are.*

Dorothy said, "We have come to meet you and see if you would be able to help us get our women's group organized and started again." She explained how the women had worked with the previous PCV, Cecelia, to start an IGA (Income Generating Activity). Cecelia had taught the women how to make batik-dyed chitenges. These chitenges sold well in the market. However, the company that sold the material suitable for dyeing had gone out of business, and the women did not know where to get more material. The cloth they needed was a heavy white cotton. The women had plenty of dye and the equipment for dyeing the cloth, just no suitable cloth.

Dorothy, the president of the women's group

I assured the women I would do what I could to help them. We made arrangements for me to meet the rest of the women's group. There were twenty-five in all. They said they would bring a sample of the dyed chitenjes to the meeting, so I could have an idea of the kind of material they needed.

At the meeting I was very impressed with the beauty of the chitenjes. A lovely, mottled, blue one caught my eye in particular. Blue is my favorite color. Judging by other chitenje's I had seen on

Malawian women, the women loved bright colors and had a discerning eye for mixing and matching colors.

We talked about what the women wanted to do. Using what I had learned in my Peace Corps training, I suggested we become organized with a proper charter and by-laws, and become registered with the Community Development person, a Mrs. Phiri, in Ntcheu. This way we would be seen as a legitimate organization, and if any information or money became available we would be entitled to a share. In the meantime, Dorothy and I would go to Lilongwe and Blantyre to see whether we could find the material they needed.

After several futile trips, we concluded the material was no longer being manufactured, and the women needed to think of another project for their IGA. I contacted Mrs. Phiri and asked her to visit us and give us some guidance. The women had decided that they would embroider and sell chair covers at the market. Mrs. Phiri helped them cut out the chair covers, and I helped by drawing patterns for them to embroider. For the next several weeks, when the women gathered in the Community Center, they sat on the floor and embroidered the chair pieces and chatted during the meeting.

Women sewing on the chair sets

Two of the women had small children. I was a nervous wreck when they took the tiny ones off their backs and allowed them to play with pointed pencils, scissors, and other dangerous things as the mothers sewed, seemingly unaware that a toddler could fall on a pencil or a sharp pair of scissors and put out an eye. Preventative maintenance was a concept the mothers did not seem to understand. I brought some safe toys from my house so I could feel less hyper-vigilant during these sewing sessions.

The women made several chair sets. Some of the sets consisted of twenty pieces. They sold the sets at the market. If a buyer wanted more matching pieces, the women would hurry home and make the extra sets. I pointed out that they were not making enough profit on their chair sets. By the time they bought the material, thread, and yarn to crochet an edging, they were practically giving them away. They were not reimbursing themselves for their time. I do not think the women valued their time, and did not count it as part of the cost of the chair sets. I could see that their efforts were not going to generate the income they wanted.

What could the women do that would be sustainable, economical to make, would match their talents, and could be easily marketed? I was aware of projects women's groups in other villages were making, such as making soap, weaving baskets, making knitted caps, or crocheting various articles. My women did not seem interested. What could my women do that was different? Was unique?

The answer came in a package my daughter sent me. The package contained several patterns of children's clothes and lots of cloth remnants. One pattern was for a brown cloth doll, about 18 inches high; just the right size for a little girl to carry on her back instead of the discarded sandal that I had seen little girls playing with, pretending it was their baby. I decided to make a doll and see what the women thought of it as a project.

I made a brown cloth doll, and dressed it with a green school uniform and a white blouse like the ones we were making for the little pre-school girls.

Sample doll on my sofa with my namesake, Melva Jane

I made black yarn braids with bangs for hair, and embroidered the nose, eyes, and mouth on the brown face. I made little panties with elastic in the waist and legs. The body of the doll was stuffed with chippings (shredded foam rubber). The doll was the size of a four-month-old baby.

The next time the women met, I showed them the doll and explained that the clothes could be removed and washed, and the entire doll could be washed and hung on a clothes line in the sun to dry.

The women admired the doll. I wondered whether they had the skills needed to replicate the doll. The dress had tiny puffed sleeves with a button placket at the neck. The blouse had buttons in the front and a collar. I worried that I was asking them to do something beyond their talents. I did not want to set them up for failure.

I told them I had visited several stores and none of the stores had dolls that looked like the children in Malawi. Most of the dolls I saw were celluloid white dolls with stringy blonde wigs and clothes that would disintegrate in water if a child tried to wash them.

Dorothy said, "But we like the white dolls."

I replied, "That's because you do not have brown dolls in your stores to choose from. Every little girl deserves a doll that looks like her."

I thought my idea was original, but learned later that a Peace Corps Volunteer in another country was promoting the same idea. Having a doll with a brown face reminded me of the "black is beautiful" concept that was promoted by Dr. Robert Cole in his research on the self-concept of black children during the Civil Rights movement in American in the 50's and 60's.

The more the women thought about making brown dolls, the more they liked the idea. I told them of a woman in Malanda, Janet, who made and sold her dolls in the gift shop at the airport and was able to provide her family with a better standard of living. The dolls Janet made were for tourists, and were not baby dolls. They were women dressed in traditional chitenjes, with colorful head scarves to match.

Once the decision was made to make baby dolls, Dorothy took charge. She soon mastered the sewing machine. She stitched the body of the dolls, and other women stuffed the body. Some women embroidered the faces, and others made the yarn wigs. One of the women, Mrs. Jackson, made a wig of yarn with a crewel needle that was then stitched on to the head. The needle created loops that looked exactly like the tight nappy hair found on the Malawian children when their hair was cut very short.

I continued to make the first dresses and panties. I made two tiny buttonholes at the back placket and stitched on two tiny buttons. I thought I would probably have to make the dresses with the tiny puffed sleeves and the little buttonholes. I did not trust the women to be able to do this. How little faith I had in them! When I was busy with something else, they kept on cutting out dresses, sewing them, and made the little buttonholes ever bit as nice, or perhaps nicer, than mine! A humbling lesson learned!

The women were so proud of their accomplishments as they lined the dolls up on Mary's bed for viewing. There were ten dolls sitting on the bed when my counterpart came in to see what the women were doing. He saw the dolls all in a row and said, "Who do these belong to?"

One woman said proudly, "They are ours!"

He remarked, in a mock serious voice, "Haven't you ever heard of family planning?" We all had a good laugh at his humor. Family planning was a serious topic at the Health Centre.

Once, when Dorothy was away, to keep the women occupied, I gave each woman a cloth doll face to embroider and explained the colors they needed to use, supplying them with the appropriate colors of embroidery floss. When the women returned the faces I was horrified. Some of the faces had green lips, yellow eyes edged in red, etc. I thought, *These faces are ruined! What could I do with them? How will I handle this situation without hurting the feelings of the women?* I was perplexed as to where they got the yellow and green embroidery floss. I had given them brown, black, and red.

When Dorothy returned, she decided to use the creative faces made by the women, but stressed to them to make future doll faces with the proper colors. She completed the rest of the dolls. We took the dolls to the IWAM (International Women's Association of Malawi) bazaar and sold every doll.

The little white girls, daughters of Embassy staff, who bought the dolls, did not seem to notice the green lips and yellow eyes. They were fascinated with the fact that the clothes, especially the panties, could be removed and washed!

Another lesson learned!

Dolls with green eyes and yellow lips

Each year, the women took their dolls to the IWAM bazaar, but were disappointed in the bazaar as a profitable market for their dolls. They took their dolls to regional craft shops, but had difficulty finding a sustainable market. I realized they needed training on how to establish and maintain a business. They needed someone besides me to give them this training. I was too busy with other things.

Dorothy's dream was for their dolls to become known world-wide, like the Cabbage Patch dolls or the Barbie dolls. I did not discourage them in their dream. It sounded outlandish to me, but who was I to say they were unrealistic? The women named their doll "Chamaso." Their translation of this Chechewa word was "You will not realize how beautiful they are until you see them with your own eyes." A small paper label is stapled to each doll's dress that states, "Chamaso Doll, Biriwiri Women's Group, Malawi Africa."

Part of Dorothy's dream was to have a building, like a factory, with a store front, where the women could make their dolls assembly line fashion, and sell them to tourists and the public. But first, they needed training in developing a business, keeping records, and finding a sustainable market for their dolls. The epilogue in this book will let the reader know of the current status of the Chamaso doll.

I have sold every doll they have sent me, and returned the money to their group. I could sell more if I had them. However, the cost of postage to send them to me is too prohibitive to make me a profitable outlet for the sale of their dolls.

Wouldn't it be wonderful to enter a toy store sometime in the future and find a Chamaso doll on the shelf?

Every success story starts with a dream. Who am I to say it can not happen? I wish them luck.

Chapter Twelve

A Visit from a Dignitary, the American Ambassador

The telephone rang. It seldom worked properly, so I was always surprised to hear it ring. I answered. It was my APCD, Edith, calling from the Peace Corps office to give me a "heads up" that the new American Ambassador for the Republic of Malawi, Mr. Steven Browning, would be visiting my site, the Biriwiri Health Centre.

My first thought was, *Why me?* It seemed that journalists, researchers, etc. were always stopping to visit us and take pictures.

The reason my site was always chosen for such visits, I was told, was because it was close to the M1 and there was always something going on. I could agree with that. Biriwiri was a hive of constant activity. I did not want the visit to be for Peace Corps propaganda purposes to show me off as the oldest volunteer in Malawi, or perhaps in the entire Peace Corps! I had read about a volunteer who was eighty, and still very active, but not stationed in Malawi.

Mr. Browning would be stopping at Biriwiri on his return from Blantyre, where protocol called for him to present his papers and introduce himself to the president of Malawi, Bingu Wa Mutharika. This protocol is followed by members of the diplomatic corps all over the world when a new Ambassador is assigned to a county.

Mary was dispatched to let people know we would be having a very important visitor. The women's group soon arrived, dressed in their colorful chitenjes. They were excited as a group of school girls. They brought some of their dyed chitenjes, and arranged them on a table in the Community Center for the Ambassador to admire.

I asked the women if they had ever had such an important visitor in their village. One answered, "Oh yes, Edith visited once."

I smiled to myself. The woman's answer showed her respect for the Peace Corps, and someone more educated from outside her village. I wondered if I was included in her estimation of an "important person." I do not think so. I had become "one of them," and was expected to pull my own weight in activities in the village. The women had quickly found that just because I was white did not mean I knew everything!

Edith was not able to tell me what time our visitor would arrive. We were on African time, which meant any time during the day. So we waited.

I envisioned a huge limousine arriving with a cadre of other dignitaries in shiny cars bearing the Malawi and American flags on their fenders, announcing their arrival with a flourish of horns, like on TV. Wouldn't this attention make Biriwiri look special?

I made tea for the women and we waited, and waited.

Finally, in the afternoon, the dignitaries arrived. We seldom had cars stop at the Health Centre so the fact that the caravan was not made up of limos but SUVs did not diminish our awe in having such a noteworthy visitor.

Exiting from one of the SUVs, Mr. Browning, a tall, middle-aged man,was dressed casually in grey slacks and a long-sleeved white shirt, but no tie. He appeared to be a very simple, down-to-earth man, with a balding head and a tidy grey beard and mustache. He was accompanied by a woman, a former Peace Corps Volunteer, who had been stationed in Malawi. He was interested in the Peace Corps program and its volunteers, and related to me as one American to another in a foreign land.

Mr. Kwanjana greeted the Ambassador, and escorted him to my house. A tall man, Mr. Browning, had to stoop to enter my door. Mr. Browning, Mr. K, the PCV, and I chatted comfortably in my newly-painted little living room. I apologized for the curious gecko that circled the ceiling above his head. I said, "Gecko's are just a part of living in Africa." He laughed, and agreed. He explained that his wife was still in the states and would be arriving later.

Mr. K. took Mr. Browning on a tour of the Health Centre. He explained how health care was delivered in Biriwiri without electricity or running water. The women proudly showed him the batik dyed chitenjes they had made. After about an hour, Mr. Browning was ready to leave. Pictures were taken and the caravan left. Life in Biriwiri returned to normal.

I did not hear about Mr. Browning again until Thanksgiving. In November I heard that all the PCVs were invited to the American Embassy to share a Thanksgiving dinner with the Ambassador. It was traditional, I was told, for whoever was the Ambassador to invite the PCVs to the Embassy to share turkey and pumpkin pie. I knew the young PCVs would look forward to being guests for a day in surroundings that reminded them of home. I was looking forward to the day myself.

Mr. Browning was a very hospitable and unusual host. In spite of the fact that his wife was still in the states, he opened his door to all of the PCVs stationed in Malawi; there were 140 of us. I was very impressed by his actions. He had the silver polished, and we dined on the state china; no paper plates for Mr. Browning's guests. All this was done with one or two servants, and no wife!

I wondered where he got the turkeys he served us. I had not seen a turkey in Malawi. The mystery was solved by a rumor that Mr. Browning had used his diplomatic position to have the turkeys flown from the states to Malawi by special couriers!

Mr. Browning seemed to enjoy the company of all the PCVs. He was the perfect host. He carried dishes from the kitchen and quickly refilled them, when empty, with squash, green beans, sweet potatoes etc. He carved the turkey, and encouraged second helpings. As I watched him, I realized that he, too, was away from home and family. He needed this day as much as the rest of us.

It was with regret that we learned Mr. Browning was being transferred to a new assignment at the U.S. Embassy in Bagdad, Iraq. The following year, 2004, the traditional dinner was prepared and served by the PCVs under the supervision of the Peace Corps Staff and the embassy cooks. I, personally, made 20 pumpkin pies and mashed what seemed like tons of potatoes, seasoned with garlic, while other PCVs prepared hamburgers, relishes, and side dishes for the crowd. We chopped and stirred and worked well together. There was a feeling of camaraderie. However, I was exhausted and my legs were tired from standing so long. We did not have turkey that year, but grilled hamburgers instead. No one seemed to miss the turkey, but we did miss Ambassador Browning.

Some of the more musically talented PCVs played the grand piano in the living room. The almost Olympic-sized pool was opened, and after a few beers the PCVs were throwing their peers into the pool. Their pranks did not stop with their peers. When I saw Shelia, the P.A., dripping wet from a dunking, I and several other "more mature" PCVs said adieu and took our leave!

I crossed my fingers and hoped the renegade PCVs we left behind did not trash the embassy and hamper any future invitations to share Thanksgiving at the Embassy. I did not hear any such rumors, so I guess they were soon dispersed by the Peace Corps staff. I felt for the cooks and anyone else who had to clean up after we left. I had heard that the previous Ambassador did not open the pool and sent everyone home shortly after eating, so that there could not be any shenanigans by exuberant, intoxicated, young Americans. He must have had children of his own!

The author and Ambassador Steven Browning,
outside her little house

In 2006, Secretary of State Condoleezza Rice appointed Steven Browning, a career member of the Foreign Service, as Ambassador to the Republic of Uganda.

I wonder whether there are PCVs in Uganda, and if he hosts them at Thanksgiving?

Chapter Thirteen
The Biriwiri Social Development Youth Club

Painting inside my house was finally completed. I was becoming skilled at cooking on the little two-burner paraffin/kerosene stove. I looked around and wondered what I needed to do next. I could always find something to keep me busy, but was it what I should be doing? I was sent here to design a specific program that was needed by the community. I did not do a community assessment, because Mr. Kwanjana told me what he needed me to do. However, I do not think my hot tea project was exactly what the Peace Corps office had in mind for me to do for the next two years. I had to think of something else. In the meantime, Mr. K was transferred to Lilongwe and we had a new Head Nurse, Mr. Kwenda.

I needed to make/write a plan, complete with measurable objectives, with a timeline for implementing the plan. I would need to have a means of evaluating whatever I was going to do. I had no idea where to start. The Peace Corps would be expecting me to include this information on my first quarterly report which was due in a few weeks.

A quarterly report was required every three months. A total of eight reports, one every three months for the next two years, were part of our responsibilities as a PCV. I had studied these reports and found them very confusing. The objectives we were supposed to be attaining were lengthy and not very measurable, in my estimation. I struggled to fit what I was doing into the framework of the reports. An added pressure was the fact that I knew these reports were summarized and sent to Peace Corps Headquarters in Washington. I did not want to let the Peace Corps down. What should I do?

As I struggled with my dilemma there was a knock on my door. I called, "Lowani (come in)" It was Mr. Ligogo and Gift Murutenge paying me a visit. As my assigned counterpart, Mr. Ligogo visited me frequently to see how I was doing. He always brought someone with him. I surmised this was a cultural thing; visiting me by himself was probably frowned upon.

I was so glad to see them. Perhaps they could help me. Before they had a chance to explain the reason for their visit, I told them about my dilemma. Their response was, "We can help you."

I was relieved and asked them how they could help me.

Ligogo replied, "The reason for our visit is to ask you to help us start a youth club."

I was dismayed, but tried not to show it. I could not see myself working with teenagers. Being an agogo, I thought my talents were better utilized with small children or adults. I think teenagers relate better to someone nearer their age, who is energetic and a good role model. I am more serious, and like intellectual pursuits. I would probably throw cold water on something I viewed as inappropriate, and would not have the patience needed to work with teenagers. I was judging Biriwiri's teenagers before I even met them.

I told myself, *Now Melva, you were sent here to help, and if this is what the community needs, then just swallow your misgivings and let this be the answer to your prayers.*

I needed a serious attitude adjustment!

Mr. Ligogo explained that a youth club had been started by another PCV. When she left, the club disintegrated and folded. A youth club was needed, because there were so many young people who did not have anything to occupy their time. Drinking beer, smoking pot, having sex, and getting into trouble at the market by stealing and fighting was how bored youth frequently spent their time. Gift added that they would like to form a football (soccer) team to help use up some excess energy of the youth. Football is a passion in Africa, and particularly in Malawi. I agreed to work with the youth.

We set a meeting date for anyone interested in helping with organizing a youth club or joining a youth club. The meeting would take place in the Community Center.

On the day of the meeting, I was amazed at the turnout. There were eighty young men at the center, waiting for the meeting to start. At the first meeting, there were no girls or women. Girls were kept busy with chores and childcare duties. They usually did not have much free time.

I surveyed the group and realized that many of the attendees were at least thirty years old, or older. I knew that some of them had children. These were adult men, not youth in my estimation. Should we include them when we write the constitution? What would be the role of these men? They had no jobs, and had idle time, and if we formed a club it would be the "only act in town." Not only would they be curious, but what else was there for them to do? What a challenge for us! What was I getting myself into?

After the meeting, Ligogo and I sat down to write the constitution. It was very open and simple. We made the age range from 15 to 30, trying to include as many of the people as possible. Most of the growth and development literature defines the adolescent years as ending at around 24, but this was a different culture; a culture I am sure was not taken into consideration when Erikson and other psychologists developed their theories!

At the next meeting, the youth decided what they wanted to call themselves. The name that received the most votes was The Biriwiri Social Development Youth Club (BSDYC). The name, suggested by a serious young man named Dayan Mkandawire, reflected what he thought should be the purpose of the club, which was to encourage each youth to grow into a productive citizen and contribute to the development of their community. I was a mere bystander as the youth took over the formation of their club.

Next they wanted a logo. They had a contest to see who could design the best logo that would represent what their club stood for.

Davie Zyaya, the younger brother of the carpenter, won this contest with his picture of a four pointed star. A sun rising behind one of the points was similar to the rising sun on Malawi's flag. The youth developed a chant when they met, "Be a star." A response to this greeting was, "Rise and shine."

I was surprised at the leadership and talent that I saw developing among the young men. It made me ashamed that I had held any misgivings about starting a club.

One intelligent young man challenged me. He said, "We have tried to have a youth club before and it did not last. What is going to be different this time?"

I was taken aback by his direct confrontation, but gathered my wits and responded, "Well, if I have done my job right, when I leave, you will miss me, but you will not *need* me. You will have learned how to continue without me."

The answer seemed to satisfy him. When officers were elected, this querulous young man, Wyson Lipenda, was elected president. He proved to be an excellent leader. However, he left Biriwiri after serving as president a few short months, to attend a Technical College in Lilongwe. After graduating from the college, he was hired to teach computer science at the same college. The young man who took his place as president was Joseph Kafakoma.

Gift Murutenge organized a football/soccer team, and the team started challenging other local teams. Gift seemed to be held in high esteem by the younger boys, as a pre-professional football player. He had never had the opportunity to play professionally, but was very much a "wanabee" football hero.

Wyson Lipenda and Joseph Kafakoma

I contacted my son, Randy Steen, a high school football coach. He sent us several regulation-sized soccer balls. The balls wore out quickly from enthusiastic practicing/playing on the sandy ground, which was like sandpaper on the surface of the balls. Keeping the team supplied with soccer balls was a constant problem. Randy had thoughtfully supplied us with a pump, but the life of a soccer ball on the rough soccer field was severely challenged.

As the football team grew, the players wanted uniforms. I contacted my friend Pat, back in Colorado and she researched everything about soccer uniforms, using her grandson, who was into sports, as a knowledgeable resource.

Miraculously, with the help of friends, Pat sent a complete set of uniforms for each team member. The boys had asked for red shirts and black shorts. Gift had always wanted a shirt with the number 100 on it, and bless Pat, she had a special one printed for him. The goalie had a shirt with long sleeves and long pants, just like the professionals. Knee socks and knee pads rounded out the uniforms. Each shirt had the club logo, the star with the rising sun, printed on the front.

Knowing the uniforms had been ordered and would be arriving any day from the states, we waited impatiently for them to come. On the day they arrived, I looked out my front window, and it was a Kodak moment. Eight little boys had gone to the Post Office (on the other side of the Health Centre) to pick up the precious boxes of uniforms. They marched in a line, like miniature safari porters, each with a box on his head, across the common area, through my blue gate and into my living room where they deposited the boxes, sat down, and waited expectantly as I opened the boxes.

The word soon spread that the precious long-awaited boxes had arrived, and the living room was overflowing with boys and men of all ages. In the last box to be opened, there was Gift's number 100 shirt! It was a day worthy of celebration, especially for Gift.

Gift wanted me to be present for their first game, which was a home game. He walked with me to the soccer field and carried a chair for me to sit on to watch the game. The BSDYC team dressed in their uniforms behind a sand dune and ran out onto the field in a formation, and then performed a warm-up drill that they must have seen professional soccer players do. It was very impressive.

The opposing team booed them, out of envy. This made the BSDYC team's day! They played proudly in their new uniforms and were triumphant, winning the game 2-0.

My sister Ruth thought getting uniforms for the team was a waste of money, and would discourage other well-wishers from contributing to the Malawi Fund Pat and I had started. My answer was, "You should have been there when the team put on their uniforms and ran out onto the field. They were so happy and exuberant. For the next two hours they were heroes in their village."

I was moved to tears as I watched the pride that having uniforms brought to them. It was worth every penny, as far as I was concerned. I wouldn't have deprived them of those feelings for anything.

BSDY football/soccer team in full uniform

Later, Gift and I searched the markets in Lilongwe to find used real leather soccer shoes. Most of the players on the opposing teams played barefoot. Gift and I thought we needed shoes to match the new uniforms. We found Puma, Adidas, and Nike shoes. We hoped they would last at least two years, if properly taken care of.

The uniforms were washed by the team members and hung to dry on my clothesline. When they ran out of line they draped the uniforms along my grass fence. For transporting their gear, I loaned the team the L.L. Bean duffel bag I brought with me to Malawi. It had wheels on it, and made it easy to transport their uniforms, shoes, and soccer balls. By the time I left Biriwiri there was not much left of the bag. It had been wheeled over rutted roads so many times, and lifted on and off minibuses. And the smell from the sweaty uniforms and shoes—!

I did not ask for it back!

The BSDY club continued to grow. A pledge membership card was printed, and signed by each member. The members wanted the pledge written in English on one side and in Chichewa on the reverse side as follows:

"I pledge to participate in the activities and programs of BSD Youth Club and use the lessons and skills I learn to improve my life. I will also use what I learn to become a productive member of my community."

These cards were solemnly signed by each member, after paying a small fee of K50 (around 45 cents). They were told to treat them like a driver's license, have them laminated, and carry the card with them at all times. It was the closest thing the youth had to an identification card.

Youth who wanted to become members of the soccer team needed to join the club and sign the pledge before Gift would allow them to play. Gift also required them to participate in some type of community service. They could draw water for an elderly person, take care of a person sick with AIDs, work in a garden etc.

A drama group was formed by the youth club. Street theater is a method of teaching illiterate people important concepts, like how to prevent HIV, malaria etc. The dramas seemed to be more for entertainment than to transfer information. I watched these 'thespians' carefully to see whether reliable information was included, or if it was just an excuse to dress up in funny clothes and be a ham for a few minutes.

A skit the youth gave for the club's entertainment was on the concept of 'sharing.' One boy had a sandwich which he offered to share with his friend. The friend pointed out that the half given to him was smaller. The first boy took the sandwich back and said, "You are right and took a bite out of his half to make it the same size. The second boy again complained that the bite he took was too big. The first boy took the second boy's sandwich back and after much dramatic comparing of the two halves, said, "You are right," and took another bite out of one of the sandwiches. By the end of the skit, the first boy had eaten the entire sandwich. I am not sure the concept was learned, but everyone laughed and the boys were delighted with the attention they received.

A few girls joined the club. Their mothers were concerned about the girls being around so many boys, and their concern seemed justified. I did not worry about Letia and my Mary, but the other girls seemed to use the club as a place to meet boys and were not very serious. The girls giggled and flirted with the boys.

A young man, Joseph Kafakoma, heard about the youth club and came to offer his assistance. A frail-appearing young man, he was very interested in community development. He joined the club and was instrumental in starting a pre-school. Before we started the pre-school, we got permission from the chiefs to use the Community Center as the place to hold the pre-school. We sent word to the community that we were starting the pre-school. Tuition was K150 a month per student. School started at 8 AM until 11 AM Three hours, with a tea break in between, is long enough for little ones ages 2-5.

The children could bring a snack, but tea would be served by the school. I felt guilty giving the children tea, but milk was not available and the children were not used to drinking milk. I soothed my conscience by making sure the teachers had plenty of dried milk to put in the tea, along with lots of sugar. Sometimes there were as many as forty students in the school. The children sat on reed mats while the teacher's taught in a rote manner and the children answered in unison, reciting their numbers and ABC's. Letia and Mary became the first teachers. The youth club and many community groups also used the community center. The teachers had to put away the children's equipment each day so others could use the building.

Children in Biriwiri did not celebrate their birthdays. This may not have been true for all children, but the ones in the pre-school were not even certain of the month of their birthday. I decided to teach the children how we celebrated birthdays in America. I made a chocolate cake by cooking it over water on my little kerosene stove. I decorated it with white frosting and put a few candles on it. I told Letia and Mary to try to find out which of the children had a birthday in the month, and write the birthday children's names on the blackboard. Let the birthday children blow out the candles, and have everyone sing Happy Birthday to them. The cake was served with mid-morning tea. I think the teachers enjoyed the cake as much as the children. Chewing on a stick of sugar cane was about the only sweet most of the children ever tasted.

I do not think births were registered in any legal way. The birth of a baby at the Maternity Unit may have been written in a ledger, but no one seemed to have a Birth Certificate. The carpenter did not know when his son was born. He knew the year, but not the month or date. He brought his son, Tiwonge, to school each day, but as soon as the teachers turned their backs, little Tiwonge would escape. I was visiting one day and watched Tiwonge. He edged closer and closer to the door, while keeping one eye on the teachers. The minute they were distracted he bolted for the door and ran outside. It was so funny to watch him. He was a true escape artist. Mary and Letia were used to Tiwonge's escapades and did not bother to chase him. Freedom was more important than 'book learning' for Tiwonge.

Tiwonge standing in front of his classmates

Tiwonge was very good with his hands, especially at taking things apart. One day, after school was over, Tiwonge 'borrowed' one of his father's tools, returned to the school, and took the door handle and lock apart. He proudly carried the pieces home to his father. His father shamefacedly brought the handle and lock to Mary. Mary and I got a good laugh at Tiwonge's innocence and cleverness. We plotted how we could outwit little Tiwonge and secure the door so that Tiwonge could not take it apart again. We put a second lock up higher on the door, out of his reach. Like his father, Tiwonge may remain illiterate, but he certainly is not stupid.

Prior to starting the pre-school, we had a painting party to spruce up the old building, with all the youth participating. We painted the walls blue, with a wainscot of yellow. The blackboard was freshened with a new coat of blackboard paint. We painted the floor gray, but later had to paint it red, like the floor in my house, after Mary complained because she was not consulted about the gray floor. Since she was going to be one of the teachers, the painters accommodated her.

When we had painted until we were exhausted, and needed a break, some of the youth left and returned with a bucket of mangoes in water. We sat down and lunched on juicy, sweet, yellow mangoes.

At one meeting of the youth club, the parents of the pre-school students were asked to attend and give us feedback on the pre-school. The parents seemed very pleased that their little one were occupied and would be better prepared for entering primary school. However, they wanted uniforms for their children. I asked them, "What kind of uniforms and what color?" They chose green jumpers with white blouses for the girls and green shirts with khaki shorts for the boys. They were very firm about the khaki shorts.

I thought, *Their desire for khaki shorts reflects the influence of the British tradition of wearing khaki shorts.*

I volunteered to buy the material and have the local tailor make the uniforms. The parents would need to buy the uniforms when they were completed.

Among the patterns my daughter had sent me were several patterns to choose from. I picked a jumper with a blouse for the girls and a shirt and shorts for the boys. The mistake I made was that the jumper had four buttons on the shoulder, two on each side. The shirt had three buttons down the front and the blouse had three buttons. The tailor made the uniforms, and I made over 200 buttonholes by hand and sewed on 200 buttons!

I attended the next meeting of the parents and showed them the finished uniforms. I told them they would cost K350 apiece ($2.30). One father was outraged. He said he could have had his child's uniform made for much less. His negative response put a damper on selling the rest of the uniforms. We were hoping to make a little money for the club but it did not happen. When I left Biriwiri there were still many uniforms unsold. I hope Mary and Letia took them and gave them to their students.

"Melva," Mary said, "We have Sadie's little brother in our pre-school."

Sadie is my little great grand-daughter. Her picture, the only picture of anyone in my family, stood on the bookcase in my living room. Everyone knew who Sadie was.

"Do you have a light-skinned child in the pre-school?" I said.

"Yes," answered Mary, "He lives in Mozambique. His mother must be Portuguese or white. His name is Zee, pronounced Zay."

I visited the school to see this child. According to Mary, he was very clever, a good little boy. I took his picture with my little Canon. When the picture was developed, I returned to the school and gave it to Zee. All the other children gathered around him to see the picture. Zee shared the picture with the children wearing a proud little smile on his face, as if he had just won some kind of honor. I wonder what his mother thought when he showed her his picture.

Zee in dark sweater and white shorts

The youth club wanted to have a party. I wondered what they would consider a party. The youth organized the party by themselves. The girls, mostly Mary and Letia, did the cooking. The food was the regular fare, nisma and rice with sauce (nidwo). I popped a huge bowl of popcorn. I gave the treasurer some money, and he purchased several cases of assorted soda pop at the little bottle store on the M1, and several packets of biscuits (cookies) for dessert.

A boom box hooked up to a car battery gave us loud African music. The youth decorated the Community Center with pink toilet paper streamers and balloons. Wild dancing and eating seemed to be the focus of the party. Everyone seemed to enjoy themselves.

After a few hours, I left and returned to my house. My head was pounding from the loud music. The old Community Center seemed to rock with the beat of the music and the stomping of feet. I mused, *This party is no different from American teenagers and their idea of a good time.*

I fell asleep listening to the loud music. I do not know how long the party lasted.

I do not think anyone missed me.

Chapter Fourteen
Death of a Friend

This book is dedicated to Joseph Kafakoma, a twenty-five year old man, who came to help in the Youth Club at Biriwiri when he heard about its formation. He wanted to get involved. Let me introduce the reader to Joseph. I still get sad when I think about his short life.

A quiet, reserved youth, Joseph had become interested in community development while working with his older brother, a CEO of an NGO in the southern region of Malawi. Joseph had been sent by his family to live with his brother after recovering from a prolonged illness, Tuberculosis, I was told. When a person is classified as "sick", this usually means they have HIV, but it is not talked about or deemed as the primary illness. In the months that Joseph and I worked together I became suspicious that he probably was HIV positive. He also suffered frequent spells of Malaria and just before he died he developed Shingles on his face. These secondary illnesses are indicative of a compromised immune system due to HIV.

Joseph demonstrated his leadership skills, rising to become the president of the Biriwiri Social Development Youth Club. His compassion for the elderly and children led him to support the starting of a Pre-school and begin weekly visits to the elderly in the surrounding villages.

The Peace Corps allowed me to pay a person K30 per hour to tutor me in Chichewa. I realized Joseph was not capable of doing much manual labor to earn money, but he was educated and a natural teacher. I asked him to help me with my language skills and he agreed. Every day he would walk the five miles from his home to Biriwiri to teach me. He was the most gentle, patient teacher I have ever known. Before he reached my house he would stop at the Pre-school to greet the children. He had me purchase a picture of Jesus, on one of our many trips to Lilongwe together, to hang in the school room to "watch over the children."

I wanted to share with my friend Pat my feelings about Joseph's death and what his friendship had meant to me. I wrote the following letter to her.

May 22, 2004

Dear Pat,

Yesterday I attended my first funeral in Malawi. It was an all day affair. I will try to describe it for you.

Thursday was a holiday because of elections. I was working at home making button holes on school uniforms. One of the pre-school teachers, Letia, the headmistress, came to my door with a neighbor woman, Alice. Letia seemed very distraught and would not make eye contact with me. Alice beckoned me to follow her into my bedroom. She had me sit down on the bed. She said, "Something terrible has happened." I said, "Is it one of the children?" Then I remembered school was not in session. Alice said, "It is not one of the children." I said, "It is Joseph." She said, "Yes. He died last night." I said, "I am not surprised. I have been expecting news like this."

Joseph was one of my dearest friends here in Malawi. He came to Biriwiri when he heard we were starting a youth club. He was 25, one of the sweetest, gentlest men I have had the privilege to know. I was a little puzzled by some things he did. He seemed to sense he did not have long to live. He was very thin and I knew he had been ill with TB. He pushed himself when it was obvious he really did not have the energy, but he never said "no" to anything that was asked of him. Sometimes I think he forgot to eat properly. When he came every morning to teach me Chichewa, I would ask him if he had eaten breakfast. If he hadn't I would feed him. If he stayed until lunch time, I would share what I was having with him. He was the Headmaster at the Pre-school (self appointed).

Every morning, before coming to my house, he would stop at the Pre-school and spend some time with the children and the teachers to see if they needed anything. Sometimes he taught a short lesson or read a Bible story to them. He bought a picture of Jesus to hang on the wall to watch over the children. Many times he made that tedious trip with me to Lilongwe to buy things for the school. We would go to Nando's for lunch and he would order ½ of a chicken and chips with a coke. Then on the way home as the vendors swarmed around the bus he would get juice and a snack.

A few weeks ago when I was ill he also became ill with shingles on his face. I knew then he probably was HIV positive. He also was ill with malaria at one point. When the immune system is weak or compromised with the HIV virus a person will have all kinds of secondary illnesses. TB, Malaria, and Herpes are the most common.

Joseph was in deep denial that there was anything wrong with him. He was willing to be tested for HIV when the rest of the Youth Club were tested. If he had been tested when he had TB he could have been placed on anti-retro viral medication and might have lived for many years.

As close as I felt to Joseph I did not know until he died that he had a child. His wife died 1-2 years ago and his little girl was being raised by his sister. No one at Biriwiri knew this either. He never talked about it. His wife probably had HIV because it is rare for someone so young to die. Their death is usually attributed to Malaria which is so common. Because of the stigma associated with AIDs, Joseph's death will probably be considered due to Malaria.

Thursday was spent sending word to the members of the Youth Club, the Women's group, and the rest of the Biriwiri community to let them know the funeral would be the next day at Joseph's family home. Food was collected and money from anyone that would not be able to attend the funeral. I had never been to Joseph's home. He wanted me to meet his mother when I was strong enough to ride my bicycle. He lived about five miles away.

On Friday it was decided that I could not walk the distance, so Gift (another dear friend and the father of my namesake) had a friend transport me in his truck. I knew Joseph's father was a farmer and that he lived in a seven room house. Joseph had told me he came from a long line of chiefs and I believed him when I saw how his home was set up like a fiefdom. The large seven room family house was surrounded by several smaller houses and huts with straw roofs. It was a small village. There was a pigeon house, a rabbit hutch, chickens of all colors, ducks, goats, and cows.

Gift approached a woman and asked if it was alright for us to enter the house. The woman took me into the house where Joseph was laid out in a white coffin with silver handles. The casket was shaped like the kind you see in Egyptian tombs. It was closed. About twenty women, including Joseph's mother, were sitting around the coffin weeping and keening in grief. When Mrs. Kafakoma saw me, she reached over and lifted a small hinged lid covering Joseph's face. A plexi -glass covered the opening under the lid. Only Joseph's face could be seen. After a few seconds she slowly replace the lid and continued her grieving. A few minutes later she looked at me and signed pointing *to her ear telling me Joseph had had an earache. I nodded because I had already heard that he had a severe ear ache which caused him to be admitted to the hospital where he died soon after being admitted. It was probably an abscess in the ear or on his brain.*

Women tip-toed in and out of the room staying for varying lengths of time. The room was cleared of furniture. The women sat on reed mats. Every now and then a man would come in shading his eyes and crying. Each time someone would lift the lid on the coffin then lower it again. Once a young woman got up and left the room crying, "The last time I saw him...." She must have been a sister. People passed money to Mrs. Kafakoma. She tucked the money into her chitenje and nodded her appreciation.

My friend, Alice, who had sat up all night along with Gift around a bonfire, came in crying. She started singing, and the women joined in. Mrs. Kafakoma handed her a song book. The singing continued, interrupted by a church elder occasionally who sprinkled the casket with holy water from a small cup at the head of the casket, using twig of a bush resting in the water. Everyone who was Catholic made a sign of the cross and repeated in unison a prayer. Apparently Joseph was a "lapsed Catholic," but I know he loved Jesus.

The women stayed with the body, but the men gathered separately outside where they sat silently. At times there were as many as fifty women in the room. A man came in singing then grabbed a woman by the arm and ordered her silently to get up. She smiled and when the song was finished she rose and graciously started dancing around the casket. Other women followed, and soon a circle of women surrounded the casket. All I could see were their brown calloused feet as they did a slow rhythmical shuffle round and round the casket. As they danced they sang. Most of the songs were a refrain and response.

After several hours Mrs. Kafakoma left the room and someone signaled for me to leave also. I found Mrs. Kafakoma outside and told her what a friend Joseph had been to me and how sorry I was for her loss. I do not think she understood a word I said, but perhaps the body language and the tears got my message across.

A woman took me into one of the daughter's house and I was given nsima, goat meat and relish of greens. Gift and Alice joined me. Gift told me I would be asked to give a speech when the speeches started. I hated that and just knew I would lose control and make a fool of myself.

Gift brought Joseph's brothers in to meet me. There were ten children in the family: Charles, Robert, Fred, Vincent, and Joseph. No one brought the girls in to meet me. There were four girls, but apparently they weren't important. I asked to see the father, and he was brought in. I think one son died some time ago. Robert is the "hero" of the family. He is the CEO of a large NGO. Fred was sitting an accounting exam soon. Education seemed very important in this family.

Around 3 p.m., the casket was carried out of the house by several men and placed on a reed mat on the ground. About eight women wearing white head scarves and carrying bouquets of yellow wild flowers followed the casket singing as they went. This procession was preceded by a man carrying a wooden cross. The cross had Joseph's name painted on it and the date of his death.

The speeches started. Mrs. Kafakoma came out of the house and sat by the casket. The women carrying the flowers and the man sat down on the mats. After several speeches, Gift came to get me. I stood up and introduced myself then told how I had met Joseph and a little about the work we had done together. I told how he had walked to the Health Centre everyday to teach me Chichewa. I learned many things besides Chichewa from Jospeh. I would do my best to make his dreams come true and I would miss him very much. He was a true friend. Gift interpreted for me.

An elder stood up next and with the Bible in his hand he went on and on like a fundamentalist preacher. When he was finished the casket was lifted and placed in the back of a vehicle. The women and Mrs. Kafakoma got in and the car drove very slowly to the cemetery. The cemetery was some distance away. Those who could not walk stayed behind. My friends decided I should not go to the cemetery because of the distance and because it would soon be dark.

I asked one of Joseph's brothers if I could see Joseph's room. Joseph had taken some paint I had left over to paint his room blue like in my house. I had made two blue pillows for his bed. He loved to stay in his room reading. He had borrowed the last volume of the Narnia series to read. It was laying on his night stand. I asked his brother if I could take it. Many people were reading the series. When I opened the book later, I found a drawing of play ground equipment Joseph wanted for our pre-school. Remembering out discussions about the equipment brought tears to my eyes.

There were over 500 people from all parts of the Ntcheu district who came to share with the Kafakoma family their sadness at Joseph's passing. The women stayed separate from the men. The men sat outside on the porches of the little huts. The women stayed inside the house or in the yard tending the fires over which huge pots of nsima cooked. Somehow everyone was fed, a few at a time.

I walked around a little bit to see where Joseph had lived. The sky was clear and the distant mountains were a dark blue. Joseph had told me his father had several hectares of land. Joseph had planted a large field of Irish potatoes a few weeks ago. Someone else will have to harvest them.

No one took any notice of me, the only white person at this large gathering. I could hear women singing softly some where. The people outside talked in hushed tones. Even the children were not as boisterous as usual. A respectful, sad silence hung in the air.

Gift came to find me and we started walking back to Biriwiri. At the market Gift's friend, Charles, was waiting and drove us back to the Health Centre.

Everyone who knew Joseph is still grieving. The youth are determined to carry on his work. They do not want to replace him as president of the Youth Club for awhile yet. His death is still too fresh for them.

This morning when I woke up I realized the children in the Pre-school needed to be told about Joseph. I went to the school and told the Head Mistress, Letia, to talk to the children. She agreed. I told her to make it simple and let them ask questions. "Tell them he will be with Jesus. They will understand that. That we will all miss his visits."

Sadly yours,
Melva Steen

Joseph was with us only six short months from November, 2003 until the following May. But, in those few months he left a lasting impression on all of us at Biriwiri. The day he died the picture of Jesus fell off the wall and cracked the glass. I do not know if it was ever replaced. It was three months before the youth held an election to replace Joseph as their president.

Joseph's funeral (Mrs. Kafakoma, second woman from left), and mourners at Joseph's funeral

"A faithful friend is a source of strength, and he who finds such a friend has found a treasure."

Author unknown

Chapter Fifteen
All God's Children

Children are amazing creatures. You can learn so much from them. I missed my grandchildren, so I opened my house to the children in the village. I wondered if their mothers knew where they were, and were okay with them playing in the house of this mzunga (white lady). Mary was usually around when the children visited, so I guess the mothers thought it was okay. Everyone knew Mary and trusted her.

There were about twenty children who came to visit me on a regular basis. I got to know them all by name. When the house became too crowded, I shooed some of them out onto the porch, where they played checkers/draughts and sat/climbed on my wicker furniture so much that it was mostly destroyed by the time my service was up. Breaking the furniture was not intentional. There were just so many of them wanting to see what was going on.

We were warned in orientation not to have anyone in our house. Someone might see something they did not have and would steal it. I decided I did not have anything in my house that was worth stealing, or that I could not do without if it was stolen. I think the warning probably pertained more to electronic things. Some more affluent PCVs had many expensive radios, cell phones, etc. My only such device was a little hand-cranked battery Grundig radio. I valued making friends and trusting people more than the loss of material things. My experience has always been that if you expect people to act in a certain trustworthy way, they are more likely to act in accordance. Perhaps I am just naïve. I had only one instance of having something stolen. I will share that story later.

My children in the states sent me boxes of their children's old toys. One son sent a box of toys from McDonald's Happy Meals. It was fun to see which particular toy sparked their interest. I thought Mr. Potato Head was an odd toy to send to children in Africa, but to my surprise it became a favorite.

One of my daughter-in-laws sent a box of bottled bubbles, the kind used at weddings and parties in the states. These were a real hit. I do not think the children had ever blown bubbles before. I had to show them how to blow the bubbles. They laughed and chased bubbles all over my yard.

An elderly woman walked by. She heard the noise and stopped at the little blue gate to watch what we were doing. I invited her in. She sat on the step and was entranced by the rainbow colors in the

Blowing bubbles

bubbles as they floated away in the air. I gave her a straw and showed her how to blow bubbles. After a few minutes she left and continued on her way. I wondered what she thought of this unusual pastime we were all enjoying

Most of the children did not speak English. English is not taught in school until the 4th grade. Still, we all seemed to communicate with each other. I decided that actual speaking is highly overrated!

The children ranged in age from pre-school to 6th grade. One older boy, Oscar, was around 13. He was very quiet, but observant. He loved to look at the magazines in my house. His younger brother, Innocent, liked to make things. He would go

Innocent and another child looking through a
scrapbook on author's table

through my garbage and find a box or a bottle
which he used to make a toy that could amuse him
for hours.

I did not see any store-bought toys in the village.
The children made their own toys. Tendai made a
car out of bits of wire. It had the shape of a car, with
lids for wheels. A long stick attached to the car was
used to guide his car over the ground. Tendai also
made up games to play with stones, like tiddlywinks.
He ran with a round old bicycle rim, tracking it
with a stick. I watched a tiny tot, about one year
old, in the under five-year-olds clinic, play quietly
for a long time with a peach pit. He dropped it into
his hand and passed it back and forth between his
hands. Who needs a store-bought toy when such a
simple thing could occupy a child's attention?

Oscar pretending to use my phone. Note the
multiplication table on the wall

Little girls would use a worn out flip-flop to
substitute for a doll. They would put it on their
back and tie it in place with a shred of worn out
cloth, and instantly they were miniature mothers.

Returning from one of my frequent trips to
Lilongwe, I brought back several small matchbox-
type cars and gave them to the younger boys.
The little boys loved these, and treasured them.
One day three small boys came running into
my yard and straight into the house. They were

very excited as they clutched their toy cars. With Mary's help, I discovered they were being chased by some bigger boys who were going to steal their cars. Sometimes the bigger boys would throw something that was important to the smaller boys down the chimbuzi, just to be mean. I was horrified that children could be so unkind to each other. I kept the cars in my house for a while, until the threat subsided and the little boys wanted their cars back.

Drawing was a favorite pastime for the children. The boys loved to draw buses and cars. It was amazing how accurate their drawings were. I gave each child a school exercise book, (a notebook) with his name on it. When the children came into the house, I had them wash their hands before they found their notebook and started drawing or read a story book. When a new child visited, I had one of the older children show them how to wash their hands in the bathroom. Innocent was very good about doing this. He would pour the water over their hands, and then hand them the bar of soap. After lathering, he would rinse their hands and give them the towel. One little boy could not understand where the water went. He stooped under the sink and looked for the water! After playing outside in the dirt, you can imagine how my bathroom looked after these hand-washing rituals.

After about an hour of playing, the children would start to get restless and would end their play session by looking at a scrapbook of snapshots of themselves. I noticed they could identify everyone in a picture except their own face. Then I realized they did not have mirrors in their houses, and did not know what they looked like. They never seemed to tire of looking at this particular scrapbook. When they were ready to leave, I would give each child a sweetie and send them outside to play or go home.

I worried that their mothers would not appreciate me giving them sweets, so I began to substitute raisins and peanuts. I cringed as they stuffed the sticky raisins into the pocket of their dusty shorts! One little boy in particular, Thomas, stole my heart. Thomas, would always bow solemnly and thank me when he left, saying, "Goodbye Madam." He was so sweet, but tiny for his age. Once he had some scaly sores on his head. I reported him to Ligogo and the next time he visited he had gentian violet, a shiny purple medicine, on his head. I think he had tinea capitis (ring worm) a fungus which leaves bald spots if not treated quickly. Since it is the custom to keep the children's hair cropped short, bald spots can be unsightly.

Thomas

This child's father had a weakness for alcohol, or so I was told. I wondered if Thomas got enough to eat. In orientation we were told that malnutrition was a problem for women and children, because the father ate his fill before the rest of the family could eat. Sometimes there was not much left for the children or the wife. We were shown posters depicting a huge man stuffing himself while the wife and children cowered in a corner looking very hungry and thin.

Crayons, colored pencils, watercolors, and lots of paper and magazines provided budding artists with materials they did not have in their homes. One day Ulemi, one of the children, and also my neighbor, told me Nickolaus had stolen a box of crayons. I had not missed the crayons. The children, particularly Adam and Innocent, usually put away the supplies when it was time for them to leave. I was usually in the back bedroom sewing or writing letters. The children were on an honor system, as far as the things in my house were concerned. They knew they had to leave the things so that the next time they wanted to use them they would be there.

I talked to my counterpart, Mr. Ligogo. He seemed the most likely person to deal with my dilemma. Ligogo quizzed Ulemi. Then, armed with the information he needed, they went to talk to the suspect's family and confront him. Upon their return, I was told Nickolaus had taken the crayons but had already sold them, one or two at a time, to several other children. I had to stifle a laugh at such an enterprising young entrepreneur. But, I quickly realized I had to nip this behavior in the bud because Ulemi was watching to see what I was going to do. Thievery was not tolerated in the Malawian culture. Sometimes the people would

Ulemi and Lovemore

take the situation into their own hands and a type of vigilante justice prevailed. I did not want any more supplies to walk away. Soon the children would not have anything to work with.

Mr. Ligogo invited Nickolaus and his uncles to meet in my house to talk to me. Ulemi, being a curious lad, and the "stoolie," sneaked in and sat in the corner. The two uncles sat on the couch. They were working men, at the Customs agency on the M1 between Mosambique and Malawi. Together they had full responsibility for Nickolaus. They appeared very frustrated with Nickolaus, and as they talked I could understand, but my heart went out to Nickolaus as I heard his story. Nickolaus's mother and father were both deceased. Nickolaus, they related, had lived with his agogo, but she could not control him and had sent him to live with his uncles. Both the grandmother and the uncles had tried to get Nickolaus to go to school. They had bought him a lunch pail, books, and school supplies which Nickolaus promptly sold and spent the money on I am not sure what. What did a ten-year-old boy need?

Nickolaus, a handsome, slim, young boy sat quietly, unmoved by the conversation around him. I had never noticed him in my house before. I made a mental note to be more aware of who was there when they came to play.

Ligogo asked Nickolaus to return the crayons. This meant he would have to go to the people he had sold the crayons to and give them back their money. I wondered if this would be possible, but kept silent until the meeting was over. Just as everyone was getting ready to leave I asked to speak to Nickolaus who was not looking the least bit sorry for what he had done.

"Nickolaus" I said, "When you grow up and walk down the street do you want people to point to you and say, 'There goes Nickolaus, the thief,' or would you like for them to say, 'There goes Nickolaus. He is a good man?"

Nickolaus did not respond. He did not seem remorseful or moved at all by what had just happened. As he left with his uncles I felt sad. I could imagine the future he would probably have. He would hang around the market, stealing or doing odd jobs until he was arrested and would go to jail. He had missed out on the love and guidance of two caring parents. I had used Ligogo's words in saying, "Did he want to be considered a good man?" These words were the highest praise Ligogo could say about someone who was honest and trustworthy.

Slowly the crayons were returned. Several magic markers were also returned! I had not missed them, either. This was the only incident of having something stolen that I experienced while at Biriwiri.

Shop Rite had marshmallows! I saw them when I went into Lilongwe. Shop Rite was a large modern grocery store. During my service, it gradually catered more and more to the needs and tastes of foreigners. The cost of most of the groceries were beyond the means of my villagers to pay for them. I bought a package of marshmallows and returned to Biriwiri to surprise the children with another American custom I was sure they would enjoy—a bonfire and marshmallow roast.

First I had to have something to make a fire. I started raking the dry cut grass on the common area between my house and the Health Centre. The groundskeepers had cut the grass the previous day, but never bothered to rake it. The children came running to see what I was doing and started to help me. Soon we had a large pile of grass and twigs.

Next I needed a long stick, a green sapling, which Innocent quickly found for me. I explained what was about to happen, and without any direction from me, Innocent and the older children lined the smaller children around the brush pile. We lit the fire and I waited until the fire was burning nicely. I placed a marshmallow on the end of the stick and held it over the fire until it was toasted. Innocent pushed the smallest child forward to receive this sweetie. The little one took the marshmallow then raced around the fire to stand on the other side. This routine continued without me directing it until everyone was on the other side of the fire and had had their first taste of a roasted marshmallow. I was impressed with the fairness and fair play of the older children toward their smaller peers. I would not have expected such behavior after the small car incident.

Mary joined us and had her first taste of a sweet marshmallow. She was hooked! After that she always managed to get her fair share of the marshmallows whenever I brought some home. When everyone had had at least one marshmallow I roasted another one and sent Adam to give it to his grandmother, whom I noticed had come out on her porch to sit and watch the activities.

By this time it was getting dark. The children were starting to play in the fire. They ran in circles carrying a burning twig and scattering sparks like sparklers on a 4th of July. I was afraid they would get burned. Many of them carried scars from being burned in their mothers cooking fires; it was a common occurrence for them. I raked the fire out and sent the children home. We only had one other marshmallow roast while I was at Biriwiri. Time did not allow for more than that.

Accidents such as falling into a fire were common. One little boy, the three year old son of Mr. Kwenda, the Head Nurse, fell into his mother's fire and put a tooth through his tongue. His father put a suture in his tongue without using anesthetic, while the mother held the child down. I suppose a stitch was necessary, but cringed, thinking how terrifying that experience must have been for the child. Mr. Kwenda's children were very well behaved and a delight to have visit me.

Shortly after arriving at Biriwiri, I heard that a child was ill with anemia and not expected to live. I was outraged. No child should die of anemia! I had never heard of such a thing happening. It was unheard of in America and should not happen here. I offered to give some of my blood but it was too late. He died. I did not realize at the time that he probably had Malaria.

When the Malaria parasite, which lives in the blood stream in the red blood cells, goes through different stages of replication it causes lysis (rupture) of the red blood cells, and anemia can result as the hemoglobin leaks out of the cells. It takes a medication like Quinine, given properly over a long period of time, to treat Malaria. Most Malawians cannot afford the medication, and seem to accept Malaria like a common childhood illness, similar to measles or chicken pox in the States. Flare-ups are treated with Tylenol and rest, until the fever subsides.

Malaria is a bigger problem and kills more people in Malawi, particularly children, than HIV/ AIDs. Trying to get the nationals to use mosquito nets at night was a losing battle. The nets had to be dipped in a poisonous solution every six months in order for them to be effective. Although nets were given to some families or sold for as little as K50 (less than 50 cents) the nets were often misused for fishing or sold. I tried to instill in my neighbors to bring their children into the house when the mosquitoes became active, around 6 PM, and not let them out of the house until it was light in the morning, and also to put screens on their windows. Something as simple as that would reduce the chances of the children being bitten by mosquitoes.

Spraying the house with Doom, a bug spray, before retiring is another way to rid the house of mosquitoes. Some of these suggestions require money, but just the price of a new chitenje would cover the cost. Women always seemed to have money for a new chitenje. Men could always find the money for a beer!

As I played with the children and read stories to them, I wondered how many of them would live to adulthood. I hoped none of the ones I was growing fond of would die while I was there. I did not know how I would handle losing one of them.

During the break between school terms, I offered to work with the children, teaching them English and math. The children seemed to have trouble with these two subjects. I asked Ligogo to borrow some textbooks from the school and I would play school with the children. The teacher at the primary school was delighted, and gave me texts for each subject and class. I purchased a colorful chart of the multiplication tables when I was in Lilongwe, and hung it on the wall. We played games, and the children seemed to have fun, but I am not sure how much they learned. I sent for a Bingo game and played a lot of Bingo with the children. Again, I am not sure what they learned, but we had a lot of fun together.

One day when I was sitting outside reading to the children, my neighbor came over and said, "You know they do not know what you are reading to them."

I replied, "Perhaps not, but they hear the rhythm of the words and can look at the pictures, and hopefully will appreciate learning to read some day."

I continued to read and the children continued to listen.

Very few girls came to play at my house. Girls were given chores to do at home, like carrying water, gathering firewood, or tending to younger children. Sometimes they carried them on their back while they ran and played in any free time they had. Boys did not have such responsibilities. They were free to play, unless their family had goats or cows which were their responsibility to herd.

One morning two little girls came to my house and knocked on the door. I invited them in but wondered why they were not at school.

"Oh madam, it is a holiday," they informed me. I checked my calendar and saw it was Canada Day but I did not think that was being celebrated in Malawi!

Mary came in and asked why the girls were there. I told her what they had told me. She laughed and said it was not a holiday. They were skipping school! I had to laugh also and said, "Fooled by two midgets!" I wondered what they would tell their parents when they finally went home.

Another time, a little boy named Precious came to play by himself. I knew he was the youngest child in his family. He was a darling little boy, very polite and well mannered. I asked him why he was not in school,

He said, "It is Tuesday. I do not go to school on Tuesday."

This answer seemed lame to me. I asked Mary why his mother did not send him to school on Tuesday.

Mary said, "Tuesday is market day. His mother is afraid he will get run over by an ox cart, so she keeps him home."

I know the market gets very busy on Tuesday, when people bring their wares to sell, but this child had older siblings who could watch out for him. They were not excused from attending school on Tuesday! However, Precious was so cute, and apparently, judging by his name, the apple of his mother's eye. She did not want anything to happen to him. I could understand.

There were so many children in the house at times that when some girls did come, sharing became a problem. The little girls gave in to the boys, and unless I monitored the sharing the girls were left out of games and the art work. I decided to have girls only on certain days with no boys allowed. The boys came anyway and played on the porch, tapping on the window to annoy the girls.

I made popcorn for the girls, and cut paper dolls for them to color, then returned to my sewing. I heard the front door open and went to check on the girls and found them sharing their popcorn with the boys on the porch. I pointed out to the girls that the boys had never shared their popcorn with them when it was boy's day. Taking care of the male members of their families was so ingrained in the girls that I could not reprimand them. Equality was a foreign concept for them. Men ruled in their culture.

One thing that puzzled me about the little girls was their habit of *not* tying the sashes on their dresses. When the tailor made a dress, he would put sashes on the dress and a placket with buttonholes at the neck, but no buttons to close the placket. The sashes dragged on the ground and the dresses fell down to the child's shoulders because there were no buttons to close the placket.

Cheroot, age nine, and Flora, age five, two sisters of Innocent and Oscar, came one day wearing new dresses made alike. The dresses were a bright yellow and orange print. They looked very nice and I complimented them on how nice they looked. Their shy smiles told me they were pleased with how they looked.

I noticed the gaping plackets, and asked if I could stitch some buttons on their new dresses. They agreed, and I rummaged in my sewing basket and found two buttons. I sewed one on each dress and closed the plackets. I tied their sashes. I wonder what their mother thought when the girls returned home. Mr. Ligogo said his little girl, Hilda, would not let anyone tie the sash on her dresses. Why the girls preferred to let their sashes drag in the dirt still puzzles me. But at least two little girls had buttons and tied sashes on their dresses for a little while!

Not all children were thrilled with the sight of me. Many had been taught that white people did not have any skin, and that accounted for our paleness, or that we were really ghosts. Sometimes I almost wished the children who swarmed in my house shared some of those fears, so I could find some peace and quiet. One little neighbor girl, about two years old, would wave to me from a distance, but when one of her older sisters brought her into the house on the sister's back, she would hide her face and not look at me. Some children actually screamed in fear and ran away. The older children thought this was funny, but I would point out to them that the fear was real and it was cruel to subject them to me. I remember one little boy standing beside me as I typed a letter. He rubbed his hand up and down my arm as I typed. Apparently he was testing the theory of me having no skin!

Even Innocent would not make eye contact with me for a long time. He was very intelligent and a leader among the children. I still correspond with him. Both Innocent and Oscar attended private school. Innocent was sent to summer school one summer term. I was very impressed that there were parents in my small village who were concerned enough to send a child to summer school. Education seems to be very important in his family. Hopefully, Innocent will be a good businessman like his father, someday.

When I decided to make a dimba/kitchen garden, I wanted to make it according to a book given to me by the Peace Corps. The book emphasized the need to make a compost pile at the same time. I had the seedbeds dug by Mkanda and Kafandiye, the groundskeepers, just like the instructions in the book, and had them leave one bed to be filled with manure, grass clippings, and vegetable peelings to make the compost pile. Now I needed manure to put in the bed. There were plenty of cow chips and goat droppings lying about in the village. How was I going to collect them? Then I had an idea!

Calling the children together, I explained what I needed. They were always willing to help. I gave each child a jumbo (plastic bag) and a pair of disposable gloves (these were on my list of things to bring to Malawi). Then I sent my little army of children running all over the village. When they returned I had them empty their bags into the compost pit, and rewarded them with a shiny new gold Kwacha I had gotten on my last trip to Lilongwe. It was like a game to them. To me, it reminded me of an Easter Egg hunt, as the children ran around gathering animal droppings, returning time and again with their filled bags. I looked in one bag and said, "Who is raising rabbits?" as I poured the tiny rabbit pellets into the pit. I had never seen any rabbit hutches in Biriwiri, but the children knew where they were!

The author's cushions suffered from the dusty little legs.
Keno, Eliya and Thomas

Soon the pit had the amount of manure I needed. I took the soiled gloves and bags to dispose of them. The children scurried off to the bottle store to spend their kwacha.

I miss all of the children.

Chapter Sixteen

My Huckleberry Finn of Malawi

One child in particular befriended me, or I befriended him. I guess the relationship was mutual. His name was Josta. He was about ten years old.

Josta wore a pair of shorts that had the seat torn out. His bare little brown behind was visible when he turned his back. I took a pair of khaki capri pants I had brought with me and cut them down to fit him. I offered them to him but he seemed embarrassed and refused to wear them.

Josta was not attending school. I discovered he could not read or write. He had a terrible cough. His cough could have been due to tuberculosis, which is rampant in Malawi. I think whatever was causing his cough kept him from school, but he did not have a good support system. He lived with his grandparents on the other side of my grass fence. They did not encourage him to go to school. He was so far behind in his lessons that he must have felt he could never catch up.

I was worried about his cough. I invited him in and offered him a cup of hot tea. Josta ladled three heaping tablespoons of sugar into his cup of tea. I did not say anything. I decided the sugar would give him energy. I offered him some Jungle Oats, complete with margarine, sugar, and irradiated cream. He ate this ravenously. I asked him if he had eaten his breakfast that morning. He shook his head "no." No wonder he was ill; he appeared malnourished.

Soon sharing my breakfast with Josta, along with a steaming cup of hot, sweet tea, became a regular thing. After a few weeks, his cough went away and I could see Josta had put on a few pounds. I encouraged him to go back to school and gave him a backpack to carry the school supplies I shared with him. He left for school with the other children. The school was across the road from the market, about a mile up the M1. I am not sure he actually entered the door of the school. He may have played all day at the market, and walked home with the other children. No one ever ratted on him, so I still do not know how he spent his day.

My Malawian friends told me to be careful. Josta's grandfather was a known thief, and was shunned by people in the village. Still, I maintained a friendship with Josta and included him in our school sessions. He was very clever and seemed to learn by osmosis, just by being included. The other children accepted him and allowed him to join in their games.

Josta

One morning, I saw Josta coming across the yard and realized he had likely spent the night in an old chicken house in my neighbor's yard. He probably watched until he was certain I was stirring about before he knocked on my door. It was then that I began calling him my Huckleberry Finn. Like Huck, Josta was a misfit in his own community. He was making his way through life the best way he could.

When I was working on a project, Josta would appear. After watching me for a while he would start helping. He was very good with his hands. He had the capacity to notice how things worked. He would stick with me at a task until it was completed,

195

and then we would stop and eat lunch or dinner. I could see in him the possibility of becoming an architect or engineer, if only he could read and write.

Josta brought me fresh fruit several times. Sometimes it would be peaches, mangoes, apples, or bananas, and once he brought some huge mulberries. I wondered if Josta stole the fruit from someone's garden. I hoped it had grown wild, and being a wild child, a true Huckleberry Finn, he knew where the fruit was hidden and when it was ripe. The mulberries were the largest I had ever seen, black, and especially sweet and delicious. I ate them with my irradiated cream. I never saw mulberries growing in Biriwiri or anywhere in Malawi. I do not know where he found them. I was operating on the "do not ask, do not tell" principle. He was always so happy to please me.

Occasionally, Josta would be sent by his grandfather to ask me for a candle, or salt, sugar, or something he knew I would have extra. Once I saw Josta slip a box of matches into his pocket. I asked for them back and told him he was welcome to anything I had, but he needed to ask me for it. If I had enough of what he wanted I would gladly share. He blushed and handed me the matches. I knew then that he had a conscience. I returned them to him, because I had another box.

A year after I returned to the states, I heard from a friend in Biriwiri that Josta's grandfather had had an argument with the nurse who moved into my house and became so enraged that he set the grass fence around the house on fire. Somehow Josta was also involved, and both Josta and the grandfather were arrested and put in jail. I found it hard to believe that a child was put in jail. Josta would have been about twelve or thirteen.

I often think about Josta, and wonder how he is doing. Life for an orphan in Africa, especially an orphan who is not educated, can be a doomed life. Josta could make it if he just had someone to believe in him.

Chapter Seventeen
A Visitor from the States

Many PCVs had family from America visit, and enjoyed showing them where they lived, the projects they had completed, and introduced them to the new Malawian friends they had made.

Aaron, a PCV from my group, rented a car and bravely drove on the left-hand side of the hazardous roads, taking his father and mother to see many of Malawi's tourist sites. They visited Lake Malawi and Mount Mulanje. In Zambia, they saw Victoria Falls and went on a safari. They stayed at Nkhata Bay, where many of us spent Christmas, and toured the national parks and wildlife reserves in Malawi.

Dakota, a young Native American PCV, whose parents apparently had plenty of money, entertained many of his relatives, a few at a time. It seemed that each week he had guests—his grandparents, parents, siblings, and girlfriend. He rented a small plane. He and his guests flew over the sand dunes and viewed the sights of Malawi from the air. He shared pictures, on his DVD, of his travels in parts of Malawi and neighboring countries that I knew I would never get to see.

I have to admit I was a bit envious as the visitors came and went in the transit house. One PCV delighted in having her mother and aunt experience the "native way of traveling" by having them ride in a minibus, packed in like sardines with complete strangers, squawking chickens, sacks of grain, and crying babies. The heavy-set middle-aged women came into the transit house perspiring and exhausted from their trip, but laughing about their adventure. I could imagine what they would tell their women's group at church back in the States.

My assignment was almost over, and I had not had any visitors. Then I received a phone call from my professor friend, Dr. Euphemia Williams, who had a pen pal in Malawi. She was the only person I knew who had heard of Malawi. She wanted to visit Malawi. Her pen-pal of over 20 years had told her about his country, Malawi, and she had always wanted to see it for herself. Having me there made the perfect excuse to visit with me, and meet her pen pal for the first time.

Euphemia is African-American. We had taught at the same university in the Department of Nursing. Euphemia has a Masters in Community Health Nursing. Her Doctorate is in Educational Psychology. I knew she would be assessing Malawi from a Community Health standpoint. I was looking forward to spending many hours talking with her about what she observed. I also was looking forward to playing many games of Scrabble with her. Scrabble is a game she enjoys as much as I. I wondered how my Malawian friends would treat her. They probably would not believe she was an American.

My date for finishing my work and flying home was tentatively scheduled for sometime in July, 2005. Our flights back to America were staggered, for some reason. I had to write a final report for the Peace Corps, summarizing the work I had been doing. Then I had to decide what I was going to do with all the things I had accumulated. It was probably not the best time for Euphemia's visit, or a visit from anyone, but I was so excited to finally be able to share Africa with someone who I knew would truly appreciate it.

The weather was mild, and the rainy season was over. It was almost time for Euphemia's arrival. It was perfect weather for her visit. I cleaned my small house and thought about where I would take my guest. I knew Euphemia would want to go on a safari, but both of us were on a tight budget. I had gone with friends on a safari in Zambia and could not afford to go on another one. I arranged for Euphemia and I to spend a few days in the "bush" at an African resort off the banks of the Shire River, where Euphemia could see many of Africa's animals, especially hippos and crocodiles. I had never been there myself, but had heard many good things about it from my more adventurous PCV peers.

On June 4th, 2005, I met Euphemia at the Lilongwe airport, and gave her a big hug. At last I had a visitor! We collected her luggage and took a taxi back into the city.

Dr. Euphemia Williams

We went first to the transit house, a place for PCVs to stay when they are in Lilongwe on business.

Euphemia remembers the transit house and her arrival in Lilongwe in her journal as:

Interesting! We slept in a room with three bunk beds six people of both genders in each room. We had to get clean sheets and make our own bed. I met several other PCVs. We walked to the Korean Gardens for our evening meal. The next day, June 5th, we walked into the town and stopped

at a tourist place that sells hand-carved wooden statues,
animals, masks, etc. I spotted a lovely hand carved chess
set. It was made entirely out of Malachite. The board
was hexagon-shaped, with green pieces delicately carved
and resplendent in the morning sun, a true work of art.
The vendor was asking $95 for the set. Melva told me to
bargain with him. It was expected. I did, and finally paid
$45 for the set. I was very happy with my first purchase in
Malawi. I recognized the value of the Malachite, although
I knew it would be heavy in my suitcase!

Pleased with her purchase, we continued to
shop for the things on my list that I needed to
take back to Biriwiri. I estimated I walked at least
six miles each time I came into Lilongwe to shop
and run errands. Thank goodness for my sensible
shoes! I do not think the Tevas worn by most PCVs
would have lasted. When I was finished shopping,
we returned to the transit house only to find it
full. It was getting dusk, so we went to the Korean
Gardens to spend the night before going to Biriwiri
the next day.

Travel at night is too dangerous, especially if
you're traveling alone. I always planned my trips
into Lilongwe so I would be home before dark.
If something happened to delay me, and I was
traveling alone, I spent the night at the transit house
and left for Biriwiri the next morning. I certainly
did not want anything to happen to Euphemia.

I wanted her to have a good experience, and learn to love Malawi as much as I.

The only room available at the Korean Gardens had one bed. Euphemia and I bunked together, and it was not to be the last time we had to bunk together!

The next morning after a hearty Korean breakfast, consisting of a smorgasbord of eggs cooked to order by a chef in a white hat and coat, sausage, hash browns, toast, jam, juice, fresh fruit, and coffee, we took a taxi to the area where the buses collect to pick up passengers for various parts of the country. The taxi drivers were always good about seeing to it that I got on the proper bus. There must have been at least fifty buses, packed like sardines in the bus area. It is difficult to decide which one goes where and when. It is organized chaos. Thieves try to grab your bags, and vendors push their wares or block your way. I was always grateful for helpful taxi drivers.

Euphemia journaled about her first bus ride:

The bus was packed, with five seats across, including fold-out seats that blocked the aisle. Melva had a lot of stuff she was taking back to Biriwiri. She had to pay for two extra seats for our bags and luggage. The two-hour ride was filled with quite an array of body odors that wafted back to us, sitting on the back seat of the bus. I was thankful for windows. When we arrived in Biriwiri, we had to hand our luggage out through the back window and climb our way over people to exit the bus. We were met by a horde of lively village children, who helped carry our bags to Melva's house.

I appreciated the children helping us with our "katunda" (parcels and luggage). They love to help, and of course they hope I have brought some sweeties for them, which I always do.

A later entry from Euphemia's journal:

Melva's house is like Grand Central Station! Everyone comes by. The children are in and out. I have met Dorothy, who makes the dolls, and Mary, who is Melva's helper. I have met Mr. Ligogo, Melva's counterpart, and Mr. Mkanda. These two men come by everyday to check on Melva.

I have started to learn Chichewa phrases. The people are pleased and amused with my attempts. I get teased! Everyone is great! I met Alice, who is going to become a pen pal. It gets dark early, at around 6 P.M. We are in bed by 7-8 P.M. Daylight arrives at 5-6 A.M. I feel like I am living in my early childhood, no running water, oil lamps, candlelight, and oil stoves! I ate nsima (porridge) for the first time. I watched Mary prepare mustard greens for supper, and learned a new way to cook greens, with onions and tomatoes. It was delicious. Mary did the laundry today, in cold water. The clothes did not finish drying by evening, so we brought them inside to dry on a wooden rack Melva got from the Vermont Country Store in America.

I found many helpful things in the *Vermont Country Store Catalog,* which specializes in things that people living in remote areas without electricity need. The things I purchased were easily shipped to me in Biriwiri, such as a washboard, a weighted drop screen door, wooden drying rack, and a soapstone soap dish. This soap dish kept the soap dry after being used by many small hands. It was a blessing.

June 9th, 2005, Euphemia is having trouble getting oriented:

I am having trouble sleeping, between the loud music from a bottle shop and the chickens waking me up so early. I am disoriented, because the East really feels like West to me. Maybe it is because I am on the other side of the world! The stars at night are so bright with no street lights to hide them. I see stars that I do not recognize. They are like diamonds sprinkled in the dark sky. The dawn is beautiful, as its red streaks spread over the sky.

Euphemia visited the clinic for mothers and their children under the age of five. The women welcomed Euphemia, and voted on a name for her. They agreed to name her Namphiri, which means "little mountain." Euphemia is not very tall, approximately 5 feet, but is powerful and strong in spite of her small body. The name seemed very fitting. She was pleased, and felt honored.

Nearly every night, Euphemia and I played Scrabble. Sometimes I won and sometimes Euphemia would win. We ate popcorn as we played. We took turns taking a bath in the evening. We saved the water and used it to wash some clothes in the morning. We still do not have running water! We tried to be conservative of water, since Mary was still having to carry water on her head each day.

On June 12th, I had made plans for us to go to Mvuu, a lodge on the Shire River which conducted short safaris. We got up early and walked to the market to catch a bus to Liwonde. We waited three hours before we were able to get on a bus that went to Liwonde. Bus schedules are very sporadic; waiting is just part of traveling in Malawi. When we finally arrived at the boat dock to Mvuu, we met our contact person, Aaron, who was waiting to greet us.

The dock was rather run down, with wooden benches under a wooden weathered roof. With a flourish of formality, Aaron welcomed us and presented us with a tray holding two glasses of red liquid. It all seemed very posh to me, while the actual surroundings were rather primitive. I was hesitant to drink a liquid that might not be safe. However, we both drank the mystery juice cocktails and thanked Aaron. We descended a few rickety steps to the water's edge, and stepped into a small motor boat. We were transported to the lodge by another man, a lodge worker, Glen.

As we cruised along on a 45-minute to one hour ride to the lodge, Glen slowed down occasionally, to point out hippos and crocodiles in the water, and various birds.

The huge bull hippos made short, noisy, feinting rushes toward our craft in defense of their harem of cows and calves. After their short rush, the bull would stand glaring at us, grunting and wheezing with nostrils flared. Glen skillfully maneuvered our boat away and tried not to disturb the feeding hippos. Our boat was small and seemed very flimsy. I felt very vulnerable, compared to these huge animals, if they decided to charge our boat. I was reminded of being told that more people are killed by hippos than any other animal in Africa.

Rounding a bend in the river, we saw the lodge. It was nestled in a clearing in the forest. I was very impressed by its picturesque appearance. I hadn't known what to expect. I had never been to Mvuu before, and hadn't even seen a picture of it. Several steep steps led from the pier at the waters edge up to the lodge. The lodge was very rustic, made mostly of logs and stone. It had a huge covered veranda encircling the building. The lawn surrounding the lodge was neatly trimmed and landscaped, with a variety of native flowering shrubs.

We were welcomed by the staff, and again served fruit juice drinks before being escorted to our chalet to leave our suitcases and freshen up. After a light lunch, we joined several other guests for an evening safari at 4 P.M. We saw many different animals, including many nocturnal animals which were beginning to move about to start their nightly foraging.

I was not aware there were so many different types of antelopes in Africa. My favorite was one that was described to us as an antelope who looked as if he had sat on a freshly painted toilet seat. He had a perfect white oval on his rear. I am surprised he is not extinct by now. His white rump would make a perfect target.

At 7:30 PM, we returned to the lodge for a delicious dinner. It was all very high-class. I was very impressed, and hoped Euphemia was also, because I wanted her to have a good time with good memories of her trip.

After dinner we were escorted to our chalet. The beds had been turned down and the mosquito nets were in place. There was electricity in our room, and Euphemia was able to re-charge her mini-cam recorder. The bathroom was made of slabs of different colored stone. It was a work of art, but there was no hot water. We took cold sponge baths and went to bed.

I went to sleep instantly, but Euphemia, who is a light sleeper, was disturbed by the monkeys and baboons screaming and playing on the roof. We were warned not to leave our chalets at night, because the hippos leave the water to forage on the lodge grounds. We could hear them snuffling and moving about. Also, elephants wander on the grounds at night. I have learned to tune out the night sounds of the animals, but for poor Euphemia every little sound was new and disturbing.

We were up by 5:45 in the morning. After a lovely and elegant breakfast, we left at 7 A.M. for a two-hour safari. This time, we saw many more animals that roam and hunt in the daytime.

By 10 AM we returned to the lodge, checked out of our rooms and were ready to return to Liwonde. On the boat trip back to Liwonde, we saw many more birds. Our guide, McCloud, was a wildlife conservation officer, judging by his uniform. He was very knowledgeable about the wildlife. As we watched from our boat, a cormorant took a baby bird out of its nest and swallowed it with one gulp. The guide had tears in his eyes as we watched this raw, and seemingly cruel, example of the "circle of life." I think that if our guide could have gotten out of the boat he would have tried to rescue the baby bird. I was touched by his concern for the life of all the creatures under his protection.

June 15th,

Euphemia wanted to visit her pen pal, Benjamin, while she was in Malawi. However, she learned Ben was living in London, England. She decided to visit him on her return trip to America. She had contacted Ben's cousin, Kisco, who was living in Blantyre, and arranged to meet him and his family.

We caught an early bus and made an uneventful trip to Blantyre, where Kisco met us. Kisco took us to meet his family, and we visited for a while. Then, in an effort to be a good host, Kisco, who had a car, took us to see parts of Malawi I had never visited. We saw large tea plantations that seemed to stretch for miles. Workers in the fields were picking the tea. Kisco explained that they were pinching off the first two leaves and a bud; the soft leaves, for the finest tea. All this, of course, was exported. The tea we bought in the stores in Malawi was of a lesser quality.

The next morning, after returning from Blantyre, Euphemia woke complaining of discomfort in her right eye. She was seeing specks that were like pepper floating in her eye. I thought the specks were what are called "floaters," a common occurrence in many people. I have some in my eyes, but have gotten used to them and do not notice them anymore. They settle into the bottom of the eye when you sleep, and become noticeable upon awaking. However, since this was a new phenomenon for Euphemia, I knew it could also be the sign of a detached retina. I was not taking any chances. I called the Peace Corps office and obtained the name of a British doctor, an expatriate who was working at Nkoma hospital about half-way to Lilongwe. I called the hospital and made an appointment for the doctor to examine Euphemia at 2:00 PM that afternoon.

We boarded a minibus traveling on the M1, to the place where we needed to transfer to another bus to take us up the road for 16 kilometers into the hills and to the hospital. We were told by the Peace Corps that the last bus left Nkoma hospital back to the M1 at 4:30 P.M. With this information in mind, we left the M1 bus and boarded the bus that would take us to the hospital. We waited impatiently, and I kept looking at my watch.

The driver did not seem in any hurry to leave. I could tell Euphemia was getting more anxious by the minute. It was almost time for her appointment and here we sat. Finally, I asked the driver what he was waiting for. He replied he was waiting for the bus to fill up with passengers. I asked him how many more passengers he needed for the bus to be full. He said seven.

Aware of being seen as a "wealthy" American, I threw caution to the wind and offered to pay for the seven empty seats. The driver accepted my offer and shouted to any potential passengers who were waiting outside that he was leaving. The waiting people jumped on the bus and we took off.

The road up the mountain was rough and tortuous. It was 3:30 P.M. when we arrived at the hospital. We went straight to the eye clinic and told the nurse our story. She was expecting us. She immediately started dilating Euphemia's eye.

I looked around the area. The operating room had no door on it. I could see patients lying on stretchers with woolen blankets over them. The doctor, Dr. Metcalf, a young man with a ponytail, was going from one patient to the next doing cataract surgery, stopping only to change his gloves between patients. Some patients, who had had their surgery, were sitting outside on the ground eating nsima while sporting a bright, white patch over the operated eye. A relative hovered nearby. A nurse told me the patients would stay overnight in a hostel, and would go home the next day.

When Dr. Metcalf was finished with his surgery, and Euphemia's eye was sufficiently dilated, he proceeded to give Euphemia's eye a thorough examination. He could detect no retinal detachment, but told her to see her own doctor when she got back to the states. Euphemia said she had never had such a thorough examination, and was satisfied with the information she received. For this very thorough examination she was charged K100, or less than a dollar.

By now it was 5 P.M. and the last bus was gone. I asked the nurse, Esther, if we could stay the night at the hostel. She said the hostel was full, but we were welcome to stay at her house. I was stunned at her forthright offer of hospitality, but we had no choice, unless we wanted to sit up all night outside and beat off the hyenas.

We followed Esther up a hill to her house. Esther made us a cup of tea, and we met her one-year-old son. A few minutes later, her husband, Hussein, entered the room. When he saw Euphemia and me sitting in his parlor, he started chuckling. He said, "I was sitting in the back of the bus when you paid for the empty seats." Hussein, we learned, was a student at a Bible College in Lilongwe.

After a dinner prepared by two little girls, about twelve years of age, apparently orphans who lived with Esther to help her with the baby, we were shown the spare bedroom. Once again Euphemia and I shared a bed. I dropped off to sleep immediately but Euphemia had a nightmare (which did not awaken me) thinking about her possible loss of eyesight.

The next morning Esther and Hussein walked with us to the bus stop and we started the return trip to Biriwiri.

On the way home, the bus stopped to allow a woman to board the bus. The woman gracefully stepped onto the bus with three tiny (about 4 months old) babies strapped to her chest, two in front and one on her back. She was alone. She carried no diaper bag or any equipment. She moved like a queen as she sat down carefully so she wouldn't crush or wake the baby on her back.

Euphemia and I looked at each other in amazement.

I said, "What a brave woman. I wouldn't leave the house with three such tiny babies without someone to help, or a stroller."

Euphemia agreed and said, "How did they all survive the birth process in this underdeveloped country?"

I wondered about more practical things, like who helped her put the babies on her body, wrapped so neat and snug? She surely could not do that by herself.

All three babies were asleep. What happens when they wake? They certainly looked healthy and well cared for. I decided she was not going far, perhaps to her mother's house, where she would have help. Or perhaps Malawian women were more courageous than pampered American women, like myself.

June 21ˢᵗ, it is my 77ᵗʰ birthday, and time for Euphemia to leave for London where she will see her pen pal, Benjamin, for the first time. From London, she will leave for America. I know she will be happy to get home.

I could now proudly say I had had a visitor. I enjoyed my time spent with Euphemia, especially the Scrabble games.

I did not realize until Euphemia's visit how much I had missed having someone to talk to.

Chapter Eighteen
Cultural Differences

This chapter includes stories and anecdotes I have shared with friends that do not fit with the rest of my stories, but made my life very interesting while in Biriwiri. My friends would say, "You must put that in your book!" So here they are.

As I have mentioned, teaching about HIV/AIDs and its transmission was a huge part of our work in Malawi as Peace Corps Volunteers. Aaron, a PCV stationed in the north of Malawi, wrote a grant and received money to conduct an educational seminar for the sex workers in his district. I was very impressed with his concern and pro-activism.

I wanted to befriend the sex workers (hoolies) in my district, since nearly all of them are HIV positive. They work at the market, especially on Tuesday when the farmers and other vendors bring their produce to sell.

One of my male friends asked me for female condoms for the sex workers at the market. I did not have any at the time, and told him to invite the women to come to my house so I could talk to them. I did not think they would come, but one day my friend showed up with a very pretty young woman. He explained she had come to get some female condoms.

With my friend interpreting, I explained how to use the condoms and told her I would provide her with some which she could share with her friends, who were also working at the market. I praised her for being so proactive. I encouraged her to get the other women to join her in refusing sex to any man who would not wear a condom, or would not let her use the female condom. She assured me she thought the other women would cooperate with her. She asked several questions which I answered to the best of my knowledge. I knew she needed to be able to trust me to feel empowered to protect herself. I gave her a box of male condoms, and again told her to divide them among the ten other sex workers. I repeated my advice to her, to tell each customer he must wear a condom before having sex with her or any of her co-workers.

Dorothy was in the back bedroom sewing on the Chamaso dolls while I was talking to the young woman. I took the woman back to the bedroom to show her the dolls. She took one doll and cuddled it as if it was a real baby.

Later, I learned from Dorothy, the woman had been married. Her husband was deceased, likely from AIDs, and that she had lost two babies. I realized the doll must have reminded her of her dead babies. She must have known she did not have long to live herself. She was earning a living the only way she could. She was still recovering from a recent case of herpes on her face. There were blisters on her forehead. When the immune system is compromised, secondary illnesses, like Herpes, can break out.

My heart went out to the woman. With no marketable skills or education, selling her body was how she was surviving. I hope she was able to use the condoms and prevent any further contact with HIV clients, because each new incidence of the virus impacts the virus already in her body and shortens her life. I never saw her again.

Not all the sex workers are passive victims. Many are very businesslike in their work, especially the ones who work near Lake Malawi. They wait for the fishermen to come in with their day's catch of fish. After they have unloaded their fish and received their pay, the hoolies approach them with their notebook/ledger and show their clients how much they owe in sex services over the period of time when they had no money. These services are tallied according to how many thrusts it has taken the client to reach climax. This business acumen of sex workers was shared with us during orientation, much to the amusement of the PCVs. I think we women PCVs secretly admired their chutzpah. Now if we could just teach them to protect themselves by promoting the use of condoms, and hopefully break one cycle of HIV transmission!!

Clean, safe, drinking water, essential for life, was an on and off problem for people all over Africa. Carrying water to their homes for drinking, bathing, mopping, washing clothes etc. was a time-consuming daily task, involving many hours of the day for women. I appreciated every drop of water Mary carried on her head to keep me supplied with fresh water. I boiled my water for drinking each evening. In the morning, I poured it through a large filter dispenser, provided by the Peace Corps.

Outbreaks of Cholera were frequent in Malawi, when a water source became contaminated. Many people washed their clothes in a river while keeping an eye out for crocodiles. This same river was too often their only source for drinking water. Not all villages had a bore hole/well from which they pumped water.

Digging a bore hole for the people in their village was a task taken on by many PCVs, especially those assigned to the environmental sector. Usually, a grant was written for money to hire a drilling company from South Africa to dig a deep borehole/well and attach a pump to the borehole.

Too many people using the same borehole, or washing their clothes near the bore hole, could easily make the borehole unsafe to use, especially for drinking water. I wrote to my friend Pat and explained how problematic it was when the pump quit and how the problem was solved or not solved. I put my remarks in the form of an essay entitled:

Going for Water

Our bore hole is not working again. The pump on the bore hole sporadically quits working. It has not worked for over a week. The hospital administrator, Mr. Kafandire, hired a private company to install a new pump so that water could be pumped to a storage tank on the roof of the Health Centre, to provide water in the Centre. Everyone was very excited about this new development; having running water in the Health Centre. Since its installation, the pump has malfunctioned three times. The "private company" takes a day or two to come to Biriwiri to fix the pump. Apparently the new pump is so complex that only the company that installed it can repair it. The previous pump could easily be repaired by almost anyone in the village.

The delay in getting the pump repaired this time seems to be because the company is installing pumps at other sites and is very busy. The women and children have been walking a long distance to get water from another bore hole. Soon the "company" will leave this area to return to its site of origin. I wonder how we will get our bore hole fixed if it breaks again. This is a question everyone is asking. Shouldn't someone in the village be shown how to repair the pump?

The new pump has a huge round wheel that must be turned with difficulty. It is almost impossible for children to turn it. When the wheel reaches its apex, the children's feet are off the ground and their weight, along with gravity, pulls the wheel back in place. Pregnant women and/or women with a 30 lb. child on their back must do a lot of stretching to turn the wheel. The old pump had an "up and down" handle, similar to the old pump cars on railway tracks. It was easy to operate by women and children. Few men fetch water, so they are unaffected by the problems related to "going for water."

Going for water takes up a lot of women's day. One PCV, John, fetched his own water while men in his village watched in awe. John would point out to them that they were capable of fulfilling this tiresome task, especially if their wives were ill or pregnant. Culturally, it was considered not proper for a man to do women's work. This even extended to carrying a child or taking a sick child to the doctor. The husband waited until the wife returned to take a child to the doctor. John did his best to confront and change some of these ideas by being a role model in his village.

I decided to accompany Mary to see how far it was to the bore hole now being used by our village while we were waiting for our bore hole to be fixed.

Mary took our five gallon pail, and we started off. We walked through a garden with corn growing over our heads. Bright orange pumpkins grew between the stalks of corn. Pumpkin leaves are cooked as greens in relish. We came to a clearing and the path branched. We took the right fork and continued walking. The path was narrow and rough. I stumbled on the rocks and clods of dirt. It had not rained for several days, so the path was very dry.

We walked through another garden of corn so tall it blocked out the sun and scratched our legs. Beans were planted between the stalks. We continued walking through another small village of mud huts with thatched roofs. Children were playing in the dust. I had never seen them before. I know most of the children in my village. Women were cooking over open fires outside.

We continued walking and came to a bore hole. It was dry and obviously had not been used recently. I asked Mary why we weren't stopping there. She replied that it was broken and had not been used for 2-3 years. So we walked on.

Mary stumbled, so I knew it was not just me who was having difficulty walking on the path. I wondered whether we would stumble on our return trip, and spill our water.

Just this morning, I heard a little girl (age 10) crying hysterically outside my fence. Several little boys were watching her and laughing. When I asked what was wrong, I learned she had spilled some of the water she was carrying! Perhaps she was afraid of being punished or was crying because she knew that meant another trip to the bore hole.

When we finally reached the bore hole, several women and children were already there. Three little girls (age 6-7) filled their plastic jugs (2-3 gallon size,) balanced them on their heads, and headed off single file toward their village. I watched them go, stepping carefully over the rocks with their bare feet. They looked like triplets, all the same height.

The bore hole was in the middle of an open area. A long trough extended several feet from the cement platform where the pump resided, and ended at a pile of rocks. Stagnant water filled the spaces between the rocks, making *a breeding ground for mosquitoes. At the end of the cement platform holding the pump was a pillar about three feet high. The women rested their buckets on this cement stump before lifting them onto their heads. One woman had a child on her back. She placed a round cloth halo on her head before lifting a five gallon bucket onto her head. Balancing the bucket with one hand she squatted to retrieve a toy her baby had dropped, then stood up and walked away.*

Mary filled her bucket when her turn at the pump came. Another woman helped her lift it onto her head. The women helped each other, chatting while they worked. Carrying water for drinking, bathing, washing the plates, and washing clothes and floors takes up several hours of a woman's day. It is a social time for the women, as they exchange news about who is ill, died, had a baby, etc. They do not complain about carrying water, but would prefer to have the well closer at hand.

I was perspiring profusely when we finally reached home. My appreciation for Mary was tripled after this single experience of "going for water."

In the afternoon, the DHO, Dr. Ngoma, and the hospital administrator, Mr. Kandawiri, came by to check on my complaint about the bore hole. The DHO was very cavalier about our problem. He is known to be a great jokester, but I was not amused. Mr. Kandawiri must have read the expression on my face, because he quickly assured me he would call the "company" and would have the bore hole repaired immediately. Talk is cheap, I have found. It is action that counts. I will keep after them until the bore hole is fixed properly.

I had to laugh when both men tried to turn the wheel and found it wouldn't budge. It is frozen solid. They were surprised, and the tone of the conversation changed to one of concern. However, all they really wanted was to have water pumped into the Health Centre.

Dr. Ngoma said, "This bore hole is not for the villagers anyway. It belongs to the Health Centre!"

They were not concerned about the community, which had been using this same bore hole for years, or how far the women had to walk to find another bore hole. I had to bite my tongue at his cavalier attitude.

I invited the men into my house to discuss progress on getting electricity at the Health Centre. I am still waiting for the quotation from ESCOM. They assured me they could go ahead with the wiring inside the Centre and the houses. I have heard this process is very messy, as they punch holes in the walls and run tubing to contain the wires. I will need to re-paint my house when they are finished.

Once we get electricity, an electric pump can be installed at the bore hole and our problems will be solved. Until then, I will continue to advocate for the women, especially for my Mary, so their work carrying water is not so tedious.

Bore hole with new round wheel pump

Another major problem, as I have mentioned before, is malnutrition. Malnutrition is due to many factors. Myths about foods, like not giving eggs to children because it will make them sterile, is one common myth. Also, if a young girl drinks the milk of a cow or a goat, she will not be able to breast feed any children she may have. Eggs and milk are good sources of protein. Adequate protein is essential for growth and good health. Since there is no electricity for refrigeration, meat, when it is available, cannot be safely preserved. Fish, chicken, and mice are common sources of protein. Eating only nsima, which contains little or no protein, only carbohydrates, is not a good diet, especially for growing children. Nsima makes the person feel full and satisfied, but does not support a healthy immune system. Vegetables and fruits are needed to supply the daily vitamins a person needs to be healthy. A weakened immune system makes a person more susceptible to infections and diseases, especially HIV, malaria, and tuberculosis.

The people in Biriwiri were healthy, and had learned how to add vegetables, nuts, and fruits to their diet to give them the needed vitamins, and ate a more balanced diet. This knowledge of a healthy diet was probably due to the teaching at the Health Centre by the HSAs and nurses. Also, the market was not far away, and most of the people at the Health Centre had money to buy extra food. However, in some of the distant villages the importance of a balanced diet still needed to be taught, and many people, mostly children, suffered from malnutrition. If these people did not have their daily nsima they thought they were starving, in spite of the fact that fruits, like bananas and mangos, were hanging on a tree near them.

I had a difficult time finding enough protein to stay healthy in Biriwiri. My weight went from 146 pounds to 112. Most of my peers also lost weight. No longer able to eat "fast food," with its high fat content, they quickly went down to their lean body weight. However, most of them declared they had never felt better and had more energy.

With my weight loss, I was able to go off my blood pressure medicine. I had my excuse for not being able to lose weight while in the states, ripped away. I thought I was doomed to be a short, plump, older woman, but the change in diet left me slimmer and feeling healthy.

To keep up my intake of protein, I ate mostly beans (nyemba) and rice (mpunga). Cooked together, beans and rice make a complete protein. I also had fresh eggs (diza) from my chickens. A friend had given me some dehydrated beans as a parting gift when I left the states. I made soup with the beans, onions (anyezi) tomatoes (matimati) and a bullion cube. I was so grateful to have those beans, and missed the delicious soup when I used the last of them.

When I was able to get butter or margarine and cheese, I kept them from going rancid by putting them in my little African cooler. This little cooler was a large clay pot filled with sand. Inside the big clay pot was a smaller pot, embedded in the sand. I poured water on the sand, and the evaporation of the water kept whatever was in the smaller pot cool. A lid over the pots helped to keep the contents fresh.

Almost any vegetable could be purchased at the market. I had carrots, tomatoes, peas, okra, eggplant, corn, green beans, etc. I guess I became a vegetarian, but not by choice! I enjoyed fish and chicken when I could get it.

Ground nuts (mtedza) or peanuts were abundant, and added variety to our diets. Peanut butter, flour made from grinding peanuts, boiled peanuts, and dried peanuts were all available. Some PCVs seemed to live on peanut butter and banana sandwiches!

We were given a cookbook by the Peace Corps, containing recipes which used ingredients readily available in Malawi. I do not think some of the young male PCVs read the cookbook. When they came into the transit house I watched the things they cooked, with amusement. I am sure if their mothers had served them the same dishes at home they would have turned them down! However, even the most finicky PCV was forced to try new dishes if he or she was hungry. One PCV, Mike, ate mice roasted on a stick. I called them mice kebabs. Later, Mike became very ill from a gall bladder condition, and had to be flown to South Africa for surgery. I surmised it was from eating mice kebabs, and expected them to find his gallbladder full of tiny mice bones!

I felt sorry for Mike, because he was in severe pain. Shelia, the P.A., gave Mike a shot of Demerol, and between Amy, Mike's wife, and Shelia they were able to get him on the plane to go to South Africa. I could picture Mike being held up by his tiny wife and Shelia as he was half dragged onto the plane. He had to walk onto the plane, or the airline would probably have refused him as a passenger and made him take an ambulance flight.

I will share with the reader a few of my favorite recipes, taken from the cookbook we were given by the Peace Corps.

Basic Vegetable Relish (ndiwo)
Ingredients:
1 small onion, chopped
1 Tbs. oil
2 small tomatoes, chopped
2 to 3 cups of any greens, chopped (Swiss chard, spinach etc.)
1 cup water
Salt to taste

Sauté onions in oil until tender. Add remaining ingredients, cover, and simmer over medium heat for 5 minutes or until greens are tender. Serve over rice.

Curried Rice Pilaf
Ingredients:
1 cup medium onion, chopped
¼ cup celery, chopped
1 Tbs. margarine
2/3 cup rice
1 tsp. dried parsley
1 chicken bouillon cube
½ tsp. curry powder
1/8 tsp. allspice
½ tsp. salt
1/8 tsp. pepper
1½ cups water
½ cup raisins
¼ cup peanuts, chopped

Cook onions and celery in hot margarine until tender. Stir in uncooked rice, parsley, and bouillon cube, curry powder, allspice, salt, pepper, and water. Bring to a boil, reduce heat and cover. Simmer for 15 minutes or until rice is tender and liquid is absorbed. Add raisins and peanuts. (Makes about two cups) I never was able to find celery in Malawi. I do not think the conditions were right to grow it. I omitted the celery, and the pilaf was just as delicious and nutritious.

If I was hungry for something sweet, I made Mandasi (donuts). Women made these little sweet cakes and sold them at the market or bus stations to earn a little extra income.

Mandasi
Ingredients:
2 cups flour
Pinch of salt
2 tsp. baking powder
2 Tbs. sugar
1 beaten egg
1 cup milk or water
Oil for frying

Mix flour, salt, and baking powder in a bowl. Add sugar, egg, and milk, beat until smooth. Drop spoonfuls of the batter into the hot oil and fry until golden brown, turning once. Drain and enjoy. Sprinkle with sugar if desired.

I can not end this chapter, which has become a potpourri of memories, without sharing my experience of going on a safari. No one, even a serious-minded, work-oriented PCV like myself, would dare go to Africa and not go on at least one safari! So when three of my best friends in the Peace Corps invited me to go on a safari with them, I jumped at the chance.

Always working, (or ill from something and not able to travel), up to now, I had denied myself any fun or adventures. I had several vacation days accumulated and needed to get away from my site and explore other parts of Africa before it was time to leave and return home to America.

My friends had become experienced travelers and had visited many places in Africa. I admired their bravery at navigating new terrain, and knew that if anything untoward happened while traveling with them I would be in good hands. Kathy and Corby were both seasoned nurses. Laura was a younger PCV, very mature for someone so young. I enjoyed her company. She seemed wise for her twenty-five years, and fit in well with us older PCVs. We visited a Travel Agency in Lilongwe and booked a two day safari to the South Luangwa National Park in Zambia.

The young African tour guide who greeted us the following morning was dressed neatly in khaki shirt and shorts. He appeared to be an experienced guide/driver. I wondered whether he had ever accompanied four American women on a safari before! He loaded our katundu/luggage in the Land Rover, and we began our journey.

Crossing the border into Zambia required us to stop and show our passports to the border guards. If we needed to have our kwacha changed into Zambian currency we had to negotiate with the money changers. The money changers were not part of the government, and were a ruthless lot. My friends had regaled me with stories of how they were scammed by the money changers when they left Malawi on previous trips. Cheating tourists seemed to be a common practice when tourists are unfamiliar with the exchange rates and do not have a calculator in their backpack. I decided I did not need to buy anything in Zambia, and kept my kwacha in my bag.

After several hours of traveling on a very bumpy unpaved road, we entered a small town. Stopping at the town square, the guide directed us to some toilets, while he prepared a lunch for us. He unpacked a cooler of sandwiches, fruit, and bottles of water. We enjoyed this thoughtful repast and a chance to stretch our legs.

Continuing our journey, we rumbled over a wooden bridge. Looking down, I saw a wide riverbed that was dry except for a small mud hole. Several people were drawing water from the shallow, muddy water hole.

I thought of the good water in the water dispenser in my little house back in Biriwiri and realized how blessed I was to have plenty of clean, safe water to drink. I thought, *If that little mud hole is the only source of water for people living in this area, what do they do about bathing and washing their clothes?*

I knew safe, clean water was a problem in parts of Africa, but the sight of this tiny mud hole was a shock. I wondered whether there were any PCVs stationed in Zambia who could dig a bore-hole for them.

We continued our tooth-jarring ride, arriving at the Marula lodge in the evening. Our driver helped us get settled in our lodge, and disappeared to be with his friends; other safari guides. We did not see him again until the end of our safari.

Our cabin consisted of two rustic log rooms with a small veranda. A river ran near the lodge and we could hear the hippos snorting and snuffling in the water. A huge anthill, over nine feet tall, towered at one end of the clearing in front of the cabins. A large covered open pavilion in the center of the clearing held tables and chairs, and served as the dining hall. On one side was a long deep freezer. On another side was a bar with stools. I wondered how the people in charge kept the animals away. It was so open. I could not see any doors that could be closed at night.

A friendly little man knocked on our cabin door and introduced himself to us as Fred. He told us that he would be our guide in the morning. He advised us to stay in our cabins after supper and not venture out, because the hippos came out of the water to feed and wandered around the cabins. Also, elephants tended to browse on the grass and ate the large sausage-shaped fruit from the trees surrounding the lodge.

Retiring to our cabin, after the evening meal, I went to bed immediately. Some of my companions, hearing the sound of animals outside our cabin, quietly slipped out the door onto the veranda and fearlessly watched the big wild animals in the twilight, as they fed.

The next morning, after a hearty breakfast, Fred arrived and we started the first day of our safari. The day was hot, but we did not mind as we saw animal after animal in their natural habitat, close up.

Nearly every species had babies. There were baby giraffes, baby elephants, a lion cub, baby antelopes, and even baby warthogs. Baby animals, like human babies, are cute. Even the little baby warthogs were cute as they scurried after their mothers, tails held straight up like little flags.

Fred knew where he could find the animals for us to admire. He shared his findings with his peers by radio, telling them where he found a male lion, or a mother lion and her cub etc. He may even have known some of the animals by name! He seemed to have a great respect for the animals, and cautioned us to be very quiet when we were near, so the animal would not be frightened or become stressed by our closeness.

About mid-morning, we stopped. Fred got out of the van, looked around the area to make certain it was safe, and then told us we could get out. He opened a small folding table, spread a cloth on it, and sat several thermos' of hot tea and a jug of orange drink on the table. Next, he placed several kinds of cookies on the table. This extra little touch of hospitality was something he started doing for his clients, he said. Now all the guides were doing it.

Left to right. The author, Laura, Kathy, and Corby.
Picture taken by Fred

After supper, Fred took us on a night safari. He pointed out all the animals that were nocturnal, using a high-powered searchlight. Again, he seemed to know where each animal hunted, and found them easily. I had my first glimpse of a mongoose. We could hear the hyenas as they scavenged the forest floor for the remains of an animal kill. Once, he reached up into a tree as we passed under it, and when his hand came back down, he held a bird. With out missing a beat, he said, "And this is a night jar."

I do not know whether this act was intentional or accidental. It seemed magical to me, like a magician pulling a rabbit out of a hat.

On the last day of our safari, Fred took us to a celebration at his village. He proudly introduced us to his children, fifteen-year-old twins, a boy named Mandela and a girl named Winnie. The famous names he had bestowed on his children seemed to reflect his pride in his cultural heritage. His concern for the animals he shared with us reflects his commitment to keeping Africa's wild animals from extinction, for generations to come to enjoy.

I wondered how many of the children and friends I had in Biriwiri had ever seen the many animals that I had had the privilege of seeing, which exist only in Africa. I am glad there are people like Fred, who are caring for the animals. I do not want the animals to share the fate of the buffalo and the passenger pigeon in America, and have children know about their country's animal heritage by only seeing pictures of the animals in glossy picture books. It would not be the same as seeing them in their natural habitat.

We said good-bye to Fred, and returned to Lilongwe.

Chapter Nineteen
Closing of Service

My assignment in Malawi was rapidly drawing to a close. I had many unfinished projects, and had been thinking about extending my service for another year to see their completion and say a proper good-bye to everyone. I could see that a third year was necessary for many of us (PCVs).

The first year is spent getting oriented and familiar with the country and its people. It takes this long to truly understand what is important to the people, and ascertain what they feel they need.

The second year is spent applying for grants and other funding sources. This is a long, tedious process, and not always successful. This time is also used to get a buy-in from the people to build what the people want/need, like a bore hole, guardian shelter etc. It takes a long time to get everyone on board, especially if you're starting from scratch with a project. A few PCVs were lucky enough to be assigned to a site where the previous PCV had a project going successfully, and all they needed to do was keep it going.

The third year is when the actual projects are built and completed. A third year gives the PCV time to see whether the project they have planned with the community will be sustainable.

This is very important. Many PCV projects fail for various reasons, and the time they have spent is wasted.

A PCV, Linda Erickson, started a goat milk project in her village. She had lived in Greece and was familiar with milk goats. She ordered several goats, built a karrel (a holding pen) for them, and taught the people how to milk the goats. The milk was to be used to feed orphan babies in an orphanage in her village. These babies were severely malnourished. Extra milk was used to make Feta cheese. Malawians have a lot of myths about giving children milk that is not breast milk. I often think about her project, and wonder if it is being maintained.

Many fish ponds were dug and stocked with fish by PCVs. Fish are an excellent source of sorely-needed protein. The fate of some of these ponds, when the rainy season was light, was to allow the project to go fallow and the ponds dried up. It took a very dedicated farmer to haul water or find a way of piping water from a nearby river to maintain the fish ponds.

A project I started, which failed while I was still in Biriwiri, was making briquettes from saw-dust to use for fuel. People would use charcoal as fuel to cook their nsima, or they would gather wood from the forest. The government banned the making and selling of charcoal. It takes a lot of trees to make charcoal. However, people were still selling charcoal and it was still being used as a fuel for cooking.

To save the forests from being destroyed for firewood, I decided to try to convince the Youth Club to make sawdust briquettes and sell them at the market. I knew I was asking people to make a behavioral change to use our briquettes instead of the outlawed charcoal or wood. I did not follow the proper steps to make this change from using one type of fuel to another. People were not ready to give up using wood or charcoal. I should have enlisted the support of more people in authority, like one of their own people who worked for the forestry, a government person etc. I thought the Youth Club could convince the people to change. I did not count on the youth sabotaging the project.

With a lot of difficulty, we obtained the sawdust from a nearby mill. This required hiring a truck to haul the sawdust to the Community Center. I had thought we could use the sawdust from the carpenters' shops, but it was not suitable. The carpenters used axes and hand saws, which produced large chips, not sawdust.

We collected scrap paper to mix with the sawdust and make the briquettes. A member of the Youth Club, Jalios Mapulanga, had experience in

Making sawdust briquettes

making sawdust briquettes (again my idea was not new!) in another town. He went to the town and purchased the machine to make the briquettes. The machine looked like an old cider press, and operated on the same principle. The sawdust was mixed with shredded paper and water in a large mortar, and pounded with a pestle until it became mush. It was placed in the press and squeezed into a round briquette. When all the water was squeezed out of the briquette, it was removed from the press and laid in the sun to dry. It was a simple procedure, using renewable, sustainable materials. The sawdust from the sawmill was a continuous supply. The schools offered their old exams and waste paper. We were in business, or so I thought!

The TV (Malawi has only one station) and the newspaper came to see what we were doing. They gave us accolades for going "green," and helping to conserve the environment. The youth were very proud of what they were doing and basked in the attention from the news media. My goal was for this project to provide employment for at least two, perhaps more, people, if they could development it into a business and maintain it.

Getting the briquettes to market to sell them was a problem. I wrote a grant for making a cart that could be pulled behind a bicycle. Such a cart was demonstrated at a seminar I had attended. The grant was funded, and the carpenter made us a cart following the plans we were given. Several of the youth took the briquettes to the market and sold them for a price similar to what the charcoal briquettes were selling for.

When it came to replenishing the supply of briquettes, the youth seemed to lose interest. I presume it was too labor-intensive for them. No matter how much I encouraged them, they stalled and sabotaged the entire project. When I quit, they quit. I could not spend all my time with them. I had other things which required my attention. At the request of one of the youth in charge of the project, Eleson Kafandiye, I purchased coveralls and had the words "Briquette Master" embroidered by the women on the back of his coveralls. Eleson was very proud of his position and coveralls, but it all ended there!

The project never developed into a true business. I was so disappointed in the youth. If the project had been in the hands of the women, I am sure Dorothy would have rallied them and they would have made selling sawdust briquettes into a thriving business.

The Peace Corps requires the PCVs to attend a number of seminars during their 27 months of service. The final one is called the Closing of Service (COS). This seminar consists of a de-briefing and wrap-up of projects, and also a time for information to be dispensed about what we needed to do before or in order to return to America. It is also the last time for all of the PCVs to get together and say our good-byes.

I wrote a final letter to my good friend and mentor, Pat Spahr, to tell her about the COS conference. Pat, also a Unitarian was a generous supporter of me throughout my time in Africa. Her letters, phone calls, and frequent packages of tea and other goodies had kept me going. She also acted as a liaison between me and the UU church back in Pueblo, Colorado. She established a Malawi Youth Fund as a 501 © (3) outreach program for the members of the Unitarian church, and other well-wishers, to donate money to help me with my work in Malawi. She shared my letters and news with everyone. I think she lived vicariously through me, as if she herself had spent time in Africa. I tried to keep her updated and informed. Excerpts from my last letter to her are as follows:

June, 2005

Dear Pat,

This will be the last letter I will be writing for some time.

As I told you on the phone, we had our COS conference at this posh resort on Lake Malawi. It was a beautiful setting, almost like Hawaii. The food was delicious. It was served buffet style on an open veranda. We had soups, salads, and several entrees (curried lamb, beef, goat, and fresh fish, as well as chicken). Every day we had three different kinds of dessert, including English trifle. Somehow, this gourmet banquet got contaminated, and I got very ill with bacterial dysentery.

When I arrived at the resort, I noticed monkeys in the trees. Then I saw that we were going to be eating outside on a lovely veranda. I thought, "This is not good!"

A guard with a pellet gun tried to keep the monkeys away from the veranda. When he was not looking, a sly little monkey would nip down and steal a packet of sugar from the tables. The chefs were serving and guarding the food, but somehow contamination occurred!

I was back in Biriwiri when it really hit me. I knew it was not something that was going to pass, so I called the medical office and they sent a transport to pick me up. By then I was so dehydrated that they had a hard time finding a vein to start an I.V. I was transported to MARS, the little hospital I was in when I arrived in Malawi and got sick after home stay. I stayed five days and had eleven bottles of I.V. fluid with antibiotics before I could stop vomiting.

I was not the only person to get sick, and we had a running joke between us, bragging about how many bottles of fluid it took to revive us! I am sure the Peace Corps office was embarrassed. They wanted to make our last days in Malawi special. Edith gave each of us a key chain of a black, hand carved wooden fish. On one side was our name. On the other side was Malawi and the dates of our service—2003-2005. I still have mine and cherish it.

When I could finally keep fluids down and started eating again, I had no appetite. I was sent to the Korean Gardens. This was my 5th trip there. It was back to eating Chinese/Korean food. After three days at Korean Gardens, I was brought back to my site. I have gradually regained my strength and feel more like my old self. One thing this last illness did for me was to help me decide that I need to come home! Someone else will have to finish what I have started.

Veranda at the posh resort for the Closing of Service
(COS) seminar

When I returned to my site, I found everyone busily working on the Guardian Shelter. I took pictures of the progress. The size was staked out. Men were digging the foundation. River sand was needed. A small pile was near the site.

The next morning I looked out my window and saw a column of women marching toward the shelter site, carrying sand in buckets on their heads. Some had babies on their backs. As they emptied their pail of sand on the pile they returned for another load. As they passed the column of women arriving, there was much slapping of hands and general good humor. They were doing their share, just like ants. Bit-by-bit the sand was accumulating. I tried to get some pictures, but when they saw the camera, they stopped, put down the sand, and unfastened their babies so I could take their picture.

Today, several men made two trips in a huge lorry to get 16 tons of quarry stone. They were exhausted from loading and unloading all of those rocks.

Women carrying sand doing their part in building the Guardian Shelter

Under the supervision of Mr. Ligogo, it looks as if we will soon have a Guardian Shelter. Everyone is pitching in to help. Now all we need is electricity.

Life in general would be improved if Biriwiri had electricity. The pump on the bore hole would operate, sending water into the Health Centre and the HSAs' houses. The women would no longer have to walk a long way for water. A nearby Maize Mill would become operational, and people would not have to transport their Maize to Ntcheu to have it ground into flour. This is usually an all-day task. They are charged per bag for transport to and from the Mill in Ntcheu. And last, but not the least reason for having electricity, is that we could find our way home after getting off the transport in the dark!

I have talked to ESCOM, the electricity company, Mr. Mkandawire, Dr. Ngoma, and anyone of importance, about the need for electricity at Biriwiri. The market on one side of Biriwiri has electricity. The customs office on the other side of Biriwiri has electricity. Why has the Biriwiri Health Centre been skipped? I had watched the poles being erected on the distant hills. They marched closer and closer to the Health Centre. For two years I was told the electricity would arrive any day.

Being the impatient American I am, I could no longer wait for someone to see getting electricity to the Health Centre as a priority. I was tired of broken promises and working on African time. I did not have much time left in Africa. This may be a "Third World" country, but it *is* the *twenty-first century*! I could see that if I left Biriwiri without seeing a transformer installed, it would be many more years before electricity came to Biriwiri. I simply could not live with myself. The poles for the electric wires were now at the Health Centre. All that was needed was a transformer and to have the proper buildings wired for electricity.

After a conference with Mr. Ligogo and Mr. Kwenda, I said, "OK, you win," and wrote a personal check for the transformer. The next day a truck came loaded with wiring, fuse boxes etc. to wire the Centre and the houses. That was the fastest I have ever seen anything done in Biriwiri. I may not see the finished product and be able to "flip a switch" and see lights before I leave, but at least the process is started.

I never told the Peace Corps office what I had done, but I have no regrets.

When I tried to compile what I had accomplished during the two years of my assignment to Biriwiri for my final report to the Peace Corps, I could not think of anything that met the specific goals of the Peace Corps. I felt my role had been as a cheerleader and coach for the people to reach goals they set for themselves, but had never dreamed they could really reach them. I ended up with the following summary.

Mostly I encouraged the people to continue in school. I firmly believe the best way to help people in a developing country is to educate the people so they will know what they need to do to have a better life for themselves, their children, and their community.

Those going to school have earned their fees by doing odd jobs for me, like painting (many things were painted several times), working in the garden, building my chicken coop, etc. They are as follows,

- Gift Murutenge, is in his second term at Sky Way Business College
- Lyson Ligogo and Eleson Mkanda are supposed to enroll in the nursing program at Malamulo College of Health Sciences in Makwasa this month. Their acceptance depends upon their scores in a Science entrance test.
- Alick Kadosa is enrolled in a teaching program at the National Resource College. He is studying nutrition.
- Both Letia Miller and Mary Chitsonga are studying to take their MSCE.
- Martin Thom has completed a certificate in Customs.
- Mike Paulos is in a private secondary school.
- Ten students of Alick Kadosa's are attending secondary school.
- Emmanuel Sampson is graduating from secondary school, and is taking his MSCE.
- Twalick Mpaweni is attending secondary school.
- Francis Mdeza is attending Sky Way Business College.

- Dayan Mkandawire is finishing secondary school.
- Richard Makwinja is going to school in S. Africa.

The following have taken exams for their JCE and or MSCE:

- Gift Nkung'untha - JCE
- Eleson Kafandiye - JCE
- Samuel Kangola - JCE-passed
- Eleson Mkanda - Science test-passed
- Lyson Ligogo - Science test-passed
- John Tempo - MSCE
- Maxwell Fuleyala - MSCE, passed
- Gift Chigunkhwa - JCE
- Tisa - JCE
- Dina Kampingu - MSCE

I am waiting to hear the results of the rest of the students' exams. Most of the people taking the JCE and MSCE are members of the Youth Club, and are adults who have been out of school for several years. It was difficult for them to find the books they need to study for the tests. I do not expect them all to be successful, but at least they tried.

Several people got passports, Thom Mambo, Gift Murutenge, Martin Thom, and Richard Makwinja.

Many opened a bank account. This small act of having a bank account of their own increased their self-confidence and has empowered them. A picture ID was needed to open an account. Having an ID helps them in many ways. An ID is needed to take the JCE and MSCE. Most Malawians do not have an ID. If they were killed in an accident far from their village, no one would know who they were.

Several people earned money to take a drivers course and became licensed drivers. Having a license did not automatically get them a job, but they felt ready and better prepared, just in case a job became available.

The Women's Group is happily engaged making and selling their Chamaso dolls as their IGA. So far, they have made and sold over 100 dolls. They still do not have a sustainable market for their dolls.

The Youth Group is still meeting and playing soccer.

A Youth Alert group has been formed for youth 10 to 15, to learn about HIV/AID's. The program meets once a week, and is led by Letia Miller. The children listen, on a small wireless radio, to a 30 minute program about HIV/AIDS, and then answer questions about the program they heard from a pre-printed test. This program was devised by the Government to try to educate young people before they became sexually active.

The Pre-school is still meeting, with Letia and Mary as the teachers. Unfortunately, Sherifa died from Tuberculosis, and Blessing left when his little brother started Primary school.

The Guardian Shelter is finished, with separate rooms for men guardians (very few men actually act as guardians) and women guardians. There are three beds in each room, a kitchen, and a storeroom with a shower. The shelter is wired for electricity and running water.

The Health Centre has a transformer, and all the surrounding buildings are wired for electricity.

Some people dreamed of building a house they could call their own. I sat with them and drew house plans on graph paper. I used a tape measure to show them how big the rooms would be. I suggested that they have cement floors and tin roofs. I explained the need for large windows for cross-ventilation and letting in ultra violet rays to kill any Tuberculosis bacillus.

When I suggested to Mr. Ligogo that he have his house wired for electricity as it was being built and that he have an outlet in the kitchen for a refrigerator, he protested vehemently saying, "Oh I will never be able to afford a refrigerator!" I told him to think big and put the outlet in his house anyway.

Dorothy completed her house while I was still in Biriwiri. Others took their plans with them and are planning how they can save enough to build their dream house.

I guess one could say I planted seeds. Some day they will bear fruit. I encouraged Gift Nkung'untha to buy one piece of tin each time he got paid, set it aside, and buy another sheet the next payday. Others are following his example. Some are making their own bricks and having them fired. They have stopped looking at the entire task as monumental and beyond their means. Instead, they see how it can be accomplished in increments, step by step.

I continued my letter to Pat:

Please do not send any more packages of baby things. They might arrive after I have gone. We haven't had a baby in several weeks, so I still have a few baby things. When I leave, that project will cease. It will be nice to come home where I can thank everyone personally for all the support. It has certainly made my work here easier.

Yesterday, I attended Editar Chibwe's funeral, along with several others from the Health Centre, including Mary. Editar was one of the youngest members of our women's group, only about twenty. She had a child, age 6 or 7. Editar lived in Dorothy's village, which is about 1½ miles from the Health Centre. I found a picture of Editar in my Women's Scrap Book and took it with me. When we reached Editar's house, I was ushered into a tiny dark room filled with mourners. It took me a while for my eyes to adjust to the darkness. I could feel hands pulling at me to a spot beside the casket. The casket was covered with a patterned cloth. I identified the grandmother, and slipped the picture of Editar into her hand. She was keening and wiping her tears. She looked at the picture and cried harder, then slipped it inside her chitenje.

The mother sat at the head of the casket. She pulled the cloth covering Editar's face down to her mouth. I could see a strip of cloth holding her mouth shut. Editar had on a woolen tam on her head, so there was not much to see, but I could recognize her. She was a tiny woman, more the size of a child. I put K100 in the mother's hand, and rose to go outside.

I was hoping I would not be fed, but food is part of a Malawian funeral. I was led to a house and escorted inside to sit on a reed mat, on the bare floor, with one or two other mourners. A woman brought in nsima, relish, and beans. After washing our hands, we ate with our right hand, rolling the nsima into a ball and dipping it in the relish and beans.

After eating, it was time to go to the graveyard. The casket was carried by several people. The rest of us followed in a slow procession through a cornfield, to the burial site under some trees. Women were crying. One little girl was sobbing and repeating something over and over. I had identified Editar's daughter and could not figure out who this grieving child was. She was about the same age as the daughter, who remained dry-eyed. I later learned she was Editar's sister. No one was trying to comfort her. I wondered how children had death and loss explained to them.

Dorothy whispered to me that the program was already set, so I wouldn't be asked to speak. I breathed a sigh of relief. Then she said I would be asked to lay some flowers on the casket. Knowing this, I made myself visible to the minister so he could find me at the appropriate time.

The women's choir from the church were dressed alike in blue skirts with white blouses and white knitted hats. Blue ties adorned their white blouses. They sang and carried bouquets of pink and lavender flowers.

The casket was lowered, and several men stepped forward to fill the grave. This took about twenty minutes. At this point, the little girl (Editar's sister) began sobbing anew as she saw the pit into which Editar had been lowered being filled with dirt. After making a mound of dirt on the grave, the next of kin, beginning with the mother, were called forward to place flowers on the mound. Each person was led by a member of the women's choir. The minister signaled me by saying, "Madam." Charity, one of the women in our women's group, escorted me. We were all sitting on the ground. I got up and picked my way over the rough ground to the grave. The choir woman solemnly handed me the flowers. I placed them on the grave, waited a few respectful seconds, rose, and with tear-filled eyes made my way back up the slope to where I had been sitting. I knew it was a great honor to be included like this. I hope I did it justice.

As we walked back to the village, the minister caught up with me, and thanked me with extended hand. I acknowledged his gratitude, but I always feel my presence puts a strain on things as the people

My group of Community Health PCVs who finished their assignment. Taken at COS on the beach of Lake Malawi. They are, from left to right, back row, Aaron, Louise, Christina, Kelly, John, Laura, Guest teacher, Gavin, Victoria, Mike. Second row, Sarah, Amanda, Corby, Edith, the author, Kathy. Seated, Leslie, Hillary, Mary, Amy. Regina walked away just before this picture was taken feel compelled to include me. On the other hand, the people seem appreciative of my presence…to know that I care. It is a fine line to walk.

I regret that I did not take my tiny tape recorder to the funeral. The songs were beautiful. I could recognize some of the melodies, but not the words.

I am ready to leave Malawi. I do not want to attend any more funerals. I do not think my heart can stand seeing any more young people die. It is so unnecessary.

The 27 months of my assignment have flown by. I am ready to return to the states and be re-united with my family. It is with a sad heart that I will say good-bye to all my African friends. I have given each of them a stamped, self addressed envelope. I told them to write to me and let me know how they were doing, and I will answer each letter.

I wouldn't trade my experiences in Africa, or the friends I met in the Peace Corps and in my assigned village, Biriwiri, for anything. I learned so much about another part of the world. The people in Malawi taught me many invaluable lessons, more than I ever taught them. I was truly humbled by their willingness to take me in, share their lives, and teach me.

No wonder Malawi is called "The warm heart of Africa."

Chapter Twenty

*The Peace Corps

What is the Peace Corps? Is it still around? I have been asked these questions many times. Always, I stop and try to inform the questioner about this very worthwhile organization. I will share with the reader information that will be germane for the young person thinking of entering the Peace Corps, and also beneficial for the older volunteer.

In 1960, while speaking to the students at the University of Michigan, during a campaign speech, John F. Kennedy challenged the students to live and work in developing countries around the world, dedicating themselves to the cause of peace and democracy.

Later, as the president in 1962, President Kennedy formally established the Peace Corps program with an overall aim to promote world peace and friendship by establishing three goals which have not changed over time:

- Help the people of interested countries in meeting their need for trained men and women.
- Help promote a better understanding of Americans on the part of the peoples served.
- Help promote a better understanding of other peoples on the part of Americans.

This last goal is carried out when the Peace Corps Volunteer returns to America and shares what he or she has learned. This book is one way I have shared my experiences. In the Epilogue, the reader will find other ways I have met the third goal.

The Peace Corps is not a part of the government, but is a separate, independent, entity with its own budget and director. Conceived by John F. Kennedy after the turmoil of the 60's, it was filled with idealistic young people who wanted to make a difference in the world. The first director of the Peace Corps, appointed by President Kennedy, was Sargent Shriver, the brother-in-law of President Kennedy.

Life in the Peace Corps is not without its challenges, but if a young person wants a time between college and deciding what he or she wants to do with his or her life, volunteering in the Peace Corps is a rewarding way to spend this time.

Volunteers receive a monthly stipend for room, board, and a few essentials, enough to meet basic needs and to maintain health. Men and women are expected to work and live alongside the nationals of the country in which they are stationed, doing the same work, eating the same food, and speaking the same language. At a grass-roots level, volunteers teach and share their skills to help solve challenges that face developing communities.

The areas in which the volunteers work may vary with the problems facing the nationals in the country in which they are assigned. In Africa the PCVs worked mainly in three areas; education, community health, and environment.

The PCVs assigned to education taught in Secondary schools. These schools are comparable to our high schools in America. The classes are taught in English. Students start learning English in the primary grade four.

I always thought the education PCVs had an easier assignment. The curriculum was given to them, and they just had to teach the subject in their native language, English. However, judging from their complaints when we met with them in the Transit house, the workload they carried was sometimes very heavy, and the students were like teenagers everywhere, recalcitrant and unruly at times. The discipline meted out on the students was archaic and punitive. For a small insignificant infraction a student might be made to dig a hole, and then fill it up again. What does this teach a child? The education PCVs found themselves in a bind, sometimes, having to support a system that conflicted with their own values. For a few PCVs this was their first time teaching. I felt sympathy for them.

I was assigned to Community Health, since I was a registered nurse. The PCVs in this category were not allowed to do any actual nursing functions because of legal reasons. We functioned as health consultants, teaching about nutrition, HIV prevention, etc. Some of us worked in clinics and orphanages.

The PCVs who were assigned to work on environmental issues planted trees in reforestation projects, dug bore holes, taught about water safety and sanitation, and encouraged newer farming techniques, like irrigation, and compost for fertilizer.

Throughout each of these three areas, prevention of HIV was a leitmotif in our work and teaching. The ABC's of teaching about Edzi (AIDs) was already being taught by the Malawi government as follows:

- A stood for Abstinence
- B was Be monogamous, if a person was not abstaining.
- C stood for using a Condom if a person was not monogamous or abstaining.

This simple program for prevention of HIV/ AIDs reminded me of the Say No to Drugs program advocated in America. Neither seemed to be very effective.

The average length of assignment for a volunteer is 27 months. This includes 3 months of orientation and training, plus 2 years. A volunteer can extend his or her tour for another year if the

Peace Corps office approves it, and more time is needed to finish a project.

The average Peace Corps Volunteer is a young person just out of college. However, more retired persons who are in good health are finding volunteering and working in a developing country, using their lifetime of skills, very rewarding. The oldest volunteer, according to Peace Corps data, was 86 when he completed his assignment.

The Peace Corps pays for your transportation to and from your country of service, and provides you with complete medical and dental care. At the conclusion of your service as a Volunteer, you will receive a "re-adjustment allowance" of $225 for each month of service. If you complete your full term of service, you will receive $6,075. These figures were current for the year 2003.

Volunteers must be U.S. citizens, at least 18 years of age, with a college degree or at least 5 years of work experience in a field that would be useful in a developing country. Married couples without dependent children are accepted if both qualify for an assignment together.

Safety is a big concern for volunteers, since they live alone. No volunteer is placed in a country that has not invited the Peace Corps to help them. The country and the Peace Corps are both invested in your safety. I never once felt afraid or threatened in my assigned village. I knew the villagers would let me know if anything was happening that I needed to be aware of, and would help me. I used the same precautions any prudent person would use, and surrounded myself with persons who cared for me as much as I cared for them.

Many young people join the Peace Corps because of the benefits/credit they receive for advancing their education. There are two ways one can receive credit: The first is called Masters International; the other is called Fellows USA. Some of these programs offer scholarships, or stipends or fellowships. The reader can find detailed information on both programs by going to the website www.peacecorps.gov. Over 50 schools offer Master's level studies in a variety of subjects after serving in the Peace Corps, and/or earning credit toward a Master's degree at the same time while in the Peace Corps.

The Peace Corps is an education in itself, but there are many other benefits besides a way to earn a Masters. Each volunteer is given 25 vacation days a year, which allows a person to travel to nearby countries. Other practical benefits are that they can defer college loans, learn and become proficient in a new language, get medical health and dental care, and live a good life prior to going into the world of employment.

The final benefit of being in the Peace Corps is you will gain new friends who will last for a lifetime.

* Excerpted from: Hoffman, Elizabeth (1998). *All you need is Love. The Peace Corps and the Spirit of the 1960's*

"The only true gift is a portion of thyself."
                                    Ralph Waldo Emerson

Epilogue

It has been six years since I returned to the States from Africa, in September, 2005. Still in a volunteering mode, I joined the American Red Cross (AMC) in October of 2005. After taking the training for being a volunteer in the AMC, I was deployed to Florida in November, to help with hurricane Wilma. Volunteers were still helping with the devastation left by hurricane Rita in Louisiana. I missed that disaster by a few months. I worked with the AMC for the next five years, helping with blizzards and stranded travelers, tornados, floods, wild fires, and house fires. I taught over 100 boys and girls in the Baby Sitting Class for AMC.

In order to fulfill the third goal of the Peace Corps as a Returned Peace Corps Volunteer (RPCV) I, with the help of a good friend, Dr. Barbara Sabo, compiled a Power Point presentation entitled, *The Peace Corps, Malawi and Me,* to show to interested groups. I talk to anyone who wants to know what life in the Peace Corps entails, as well as life in a third world country.

I hear from many of my friends in Biriwiri, some by letters, but most have learned to use an Internet Café in Ntcheu and send me e-mails. Many have reached new goals in their life. Others are still dreaming, hoarding their house plans, and looking to a better future.

My namesake, little Melva, born January 28th, 2004, will be seven, and is in Primary school. Her father, Gift Murutenge, graduated from Sky Way Business College with a diploma in Community Development. I attended his graduation, the only white person in the audience. He still lives in Biriwiri, working as a farmer. He became a trusted friend I knew I could always count on.

Mr. Ligogo and Mr. Mkanda both passed their Science class. Mr. Ligogo received a certificate in nursing. He plans to return to school for a diploma in nursing. He sent me plans of the house he is building in Ntcheu. The house not only has a place for a refrigerator, but two bathrooms and three bedrooms!

Mr. Mkanda's father died. Being the first-born in his family, he has had other responsibilities, and has had to put a hold on his own ambitions.

The Women's Group received an order for 300 Chamaso dolls from UNICEF. Hopefully, UNICEF will become a sustainable outlet for their dolls. The women are the recipients of a grant from FOM (Friends of Malawi) a group of returned RPCVs, for four new sewing machines. Next they want to build a factory to house their new machines. They have received training from Towlera Jalakasi, a business consultant with Cooperation of Fair Trade in Africa (COFTA), on how to run a business. I am so proud of the women. They have worked very hard, keeping their eye on their goal of making the Chamaso doll known all over the world.

I am not certain if the Youth Group is still active, but the Junior Alert group is still meeting, under the tutelage of faithful Letia. She continues to educate the young boys and girls about the dangers of unprotected sex. Letia is still teaching the pre-school children by herself. She has built a house for herself and Clement. As Ligogo once said, "What this community needs is more committed people like Letia."

Mary Chitsonga moved to her home village at Matanda after I left. She has started a very successful pre-school for her village, hiring her two sisters to help her with the school. Pat keeps in touch with Mary. She recently sent 30 bright yellow tee-shirts, with a purple logo designed by Mary, for her students, and also matching tees for the teachers

The electricity is operating at the Health Centre. I do not know if the mill or the little bottle stores along the M1 have electricity. I wonder whether the mothers are getting their hot tea.

The Unitarian Universalist Church in Pueblo, Colorado has been very helpful in starting an Outreach Program with a contact in Malawi, Alick Kadosa. Through this program, 501 © (3) we sponsor ten Secondary students at a time, assisting them with fees to complete their education. Upon completion of Form Four, we pay their fees to take the Malawi Secondary Certificate Exam (MSCE). Without this certificate, it is impossible for a young person to find employment or advance in his/her education.

So far, we have assisted twenty-two young people in finishing their Secondary education. They have taken their MSCE, but many have had to repeat the test. The test is very difficult, and a fee is assessed to take the test. The test originates in England. The entire educational system in Malawi is based on the English model. Alick tells us the need to repeat the test is mostly due to the lack of textbooks. Pat and I are trying to get textbooks into the hands of all the students. The well-wishers, at the church and in the community, have helped us by sending to each student a backpack, a set of school supplies (including a scientific calculator), a Good News Bible (the students are tested on this version of the Bible), and an English Dictionary.

I firmly believe that the only way to help a Third World country is by educating the people to help themselves. In helping just one clever young adult reach his/her educational goals, an entire family will benefit, and their standard of living will increase.

I received a letter from a student in the Malawi Youth Program, Mestina Wellos. She states, in her own words:

"I write to thank you to keep me in school. I have learnt a lot about the importance of education. I have

learnt to need and understand English. My daily
life has changed because wherever I am I think of my
education. Your intervention has assisted me very
much because I could not find school requirements on
my own. You have also assisted our family as a whole
because most of the members are illiterate. I assist the
family when there is need to write or read."

Mestina's letter is similar to the letters we receive from our students. Helping educate students like Mestina will have a ripple effect in her family and her community. I wish we had the funds to support more than ten students at a time, so we could create more ripples all over Malawi! I am always looking for other ways to raise money to sustain and expand the Malawi Youth Program.

I would like to start a Foundation similar to Greg Mortenson's Central Asia's Institute (CAI). Greg is the author of *Three Cups of Tea* and *Stones into Schools*. A Foundation would allow us to assist the many students who write to us wanting us to pay their fees to continue their education, which we sadly have to turn down. Both Pat and I are in our 80's, so such an ambition does not seem possible.

In 2010, the Peace Corps received the biggest increase in funding since its founding in 1962. I do not know if this increase in funding will change the amounts I have quoted for stipends etc. in Chapter Twenty. Nevertheless, I think the increase in funding, despite the economic slow-down America is facing, reflects the value and appreciation the government has for the work of the Peace Corps.

The twenty-seven months I spent in Africa were not the easiest in my life, but were very rewarding. I enjoyed the relaxed pace of life. Like so many Americans, I am very time and outcome oriented.

Slowing down and living according to the rhythms of African time was difficult for me at first, but I finally adapted. My Malawians friends might tend to disagree!

I am sure I took away more worthwhile life lessons than I ever taught. My heart holds a special place for the friends I made, and the kindness of the African people to this American agogo. I am now 82, and ready to retire my sensible shoes and live with my memories.

Zikomo Kwamberi, (Thank you very much!)

"The great use of life is to spend it for something that will outlast it."

William James

Acknowledgments

This book could not have been written without the encouragement and support of my friends and family.

When I returned from my twenty seven months in Africa, it seemed I was always talking about Malawi and my experiences whether my audience wanted to hear about them or not. I am sure I bored many people. However, I justified my talking about Malawi by telling myself I was fulfilling the third goal of the Peace Corps which all of the PCVs pledged faithfully to do at our COS meeting upon our return to the states. (See Chapter 20 for this goal). Perhaps I over-did my sharing, but when I started to write this book so many people remembered my stories and would say, "Do not forget to tell about..."

In particular, I want to thank Dr. Barbara Sabo, my teaching peer, who made a scrapbook of my best pictures which I treasure. She listened to my stories, then helped me by making a Power Point Presentation for the many talks I gave to a variety of groups who were interested in hearing about the Peace Corps and its work.

My good friend and supporter, Patricia Spahr designed a brochure for the Malawi Youth Program I had started in Malawi with Alick Kadosa as the director. The brochure is just one of the many thoughtful things Pat did for me. I will always be grateful for her wisdom and assistance. Pat shared my letters and pictures at our Unitarian Universalist church by posting them on a red felt bulletin board. She encouraged friends in the church to support me with money, cards, letters and care packages.

Maria Westy Bush remembered me with her watercolor note cards of animals she sketched in Colorado. I collected these cards and made a collage to remind me of home in Colorado.

Other women in the church, too many to list, sent baby clothes which I lovingly shared with the new mothers on my tea tray. The appreciation of the new mothers was very gratifying. I wished I could have shared their gratitude with their benefactors. My sister, Ruth Hornsby, and her women's group at her church in St. Joseph, Missouri also sent many packets of baby clothes.

Love and gratitude go to all of my Malawian friends, a few of whom are listed in the text of this book. I hope I spelled their names correctly. I hope the many who are not mentioned will forgive me and know that I care about them and remember all of them fondly.

Love also goes to all of my children, Bill, Jayne, Vance, Randy, Charles and Holly (my granddaughter), grandchildren, and great grandchildren. The many packages they sent to me were enjoyed by my surrogate Malawian children.

A special thanks to Liz Moulter for her gift of the title for this book, *Sensible Shoes*. It is a title she hoped to use one day, but felt it was very fitting for my book and bequeathed it to me.

Lastly, I must thank the two computer whizzes who share my living space, Chantelle Benally and Ezzat Farahzad (students). When I had trouble with my computer they were quick to use their technical skills to get me back on track. I love both of them and am forever in debt to them.

About the Author

In 2003 Dr. Melva Jane (Dix) Steen joined The Peace Corps (P.C.) at the age of 74. She spent 27 months in Malawi, Africa.

She shares in this book her experiences of being the oldest volunteer living and working in Malawi, in the hope that others, especially older persons, will be motivated to expand their horizons by becoming a Peace Corps Volunteer.

Since returning to the States in 2005, Dr. Steen has given many talks to a variety of audiences about what it is like to live in a developing country. She has continued a program started in Malawi to help ten Secondary students, at a time, primarily orphans, complete their education and pass their Malawi Secondary Certificate Exams. She works with a Malawian counterpart, Alick Kadosa, (see page 85) who selects the students and monitors the program. This Malawian Youth Program is supported by her Unitarian Universalist church in Pueblo, Colorado as an Outreach program.

Dr. Steen currently resides in Pueblo, Colorado. She plans to move back to Missouri to be closer to her children and siblings. She will reside at John Knox Village, a senior retirement community, located in Lee's Summit, Missouri. She can be reached at melva@usa.com

This book has been typed by the author using size 14 font especially for older eyes.

Person's interested in purchasing a Chamaso doll may contact Dorothy Kasamba at dorothykasamba@yahoo.com Dorothy's women's group makes girl dolls with nappy hair and some with braided hair with beads. They also make boy dolls. The cost for each doll is $25. This includes mailing from Africa.